HOTTENTOTS HOLLAND
TO HERMANUS

The Walks
1 Sir Lowry's Pass
2 Nuweberg
3 Jan Joubert's Gat
4 Jonkershoek
5 Kleinmond
6 Bettys Bay
7 Hermanus

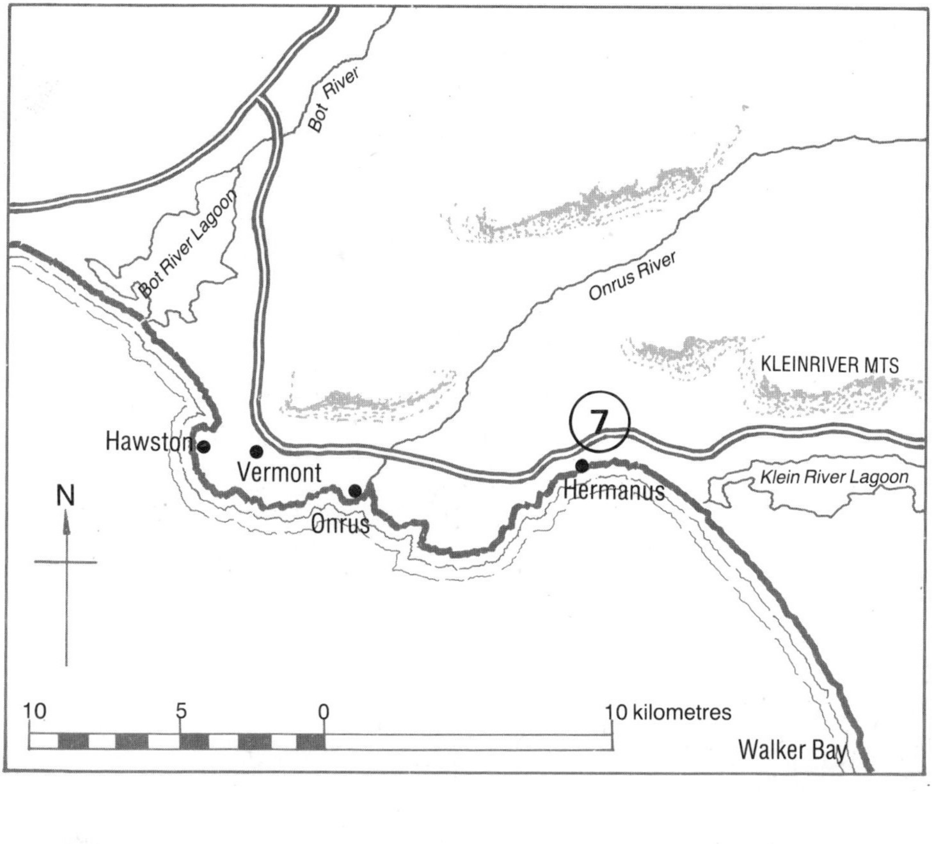

Hottentots Holland to Hermanus

South African Wild Flower Guide 5

Text by
LEE BURMAN AND ANNE BEAN

Photographs by
JOSE BURMAN

This guide is the fifth
in a series of Wild Flower Guides
published by the Botanical Society
of South Africa

The Botanical Society of South Africa was founded in 1913 to support the National Botanic Gardens and thus to promote the conservation and cultivation of our indigenous flora.

One of our projects is the publication of a series of wild flower guides.

Already published:

Namaqualand & Clanwilliam	1981
Outeniqua Tsitsikamma & eastern Little Karoo	1982
Cape Peninsula	1983
Transvaal Lowveld & Escarpment	1984
Hottentots Holland to Hermanus	1985

These and future guides will eventually cover most of the wild flowers of South Africa.

For further information about the Botanical Society and its membership, please see the inside back cover.

Published 1985
Botanical Society of South Africa
Kirstenbosch, Claremont 7735 R.S.A.

Distributed by Struik Book Distributors (Pty) Ltd.

Copyright: © Text, Lee Burman
Copyright: © Photographs, Jose Burman

Reproduction by Unifoto (Pty) Ltd. Cape Town
Printed by Blackshaws (Pty) Ltd., Cape Town

All rights reserved. No part of this publication may be reproduced, stored in a retrieval system or transmitted, in any form or by any means, electronic, mechanical, photocopying, recording or otherwise without the permission of the copyright owner.

ISBN 0 620 08393 X (soft cover)

ISBN 0 620 08394 8 (hard cover)

Opposite Title Page: *Podocarpus elongatus* near mouth of Palmiet River
Cover: *Crassula coccinea*

Message from the Vice-Chancellor and Principal of the University of Cape Town, Dr. S.J. Saunders

South Africa has a floral kingdom unsurpassed in its variety and beauty, and no-where is this better seen than in the area described in this book. This is fynbos country, a shrub-land containing beautiful examples of proteas, heaths and reeds, set in an area bounded by the sea on the one hand and towering mountains on the other. This is part of the heritage of South Africa, and it gives great pleasure to all of us to know that so many people are determined to preserve our priceless flora. Anyone who walks through the fields, over the lower hills, and explores the deep kloofs will be enriched by the vegetation which abounds in this area, and will recall the experience in later years as an unforgettable one, experiencing at the same time an irresistible urge to return again and again.

Most of us live in cities and our lives are dominated by the blessings and curses of late twentieth century urban life which makes it a real privilege for us to visit areas such as those described in this volume.

I would like to compliment the Botanical Society of South Africa for publishing this volume.

In particular I congratulate the authors for producing such a fine work, so well illustrated. I believe that it will bring great pleasure to many, and I hope that it will encourage South Africans and overseas visitors alike to go to the land of the fynbos and to savour its magnificence.

DR S J SAUNDERS
JULY 1985

Contents

Message by Dr. S. Saunders, Vice-Chancellor of
the University of Cape Town   5

Acknowledgements   9

Foreword by A. van der Dussen, Deputy
Director General, Department of Environment
Affairs   11

Introduction   13
   Geology   13
   Habitats   14
   Fire   14
   Conservation   15
   How to use this guide   17
The Hiking Trails   17
Descriptions of plants   24

Glossary   208

Index to botanical names   211
Index to common names   218

Euryops abrotanoides in the Hottentots Holland

This unique series of Wild Flower Guides is co-ordinated and published by the Botanical Society of South Africa. It is made possible by the co-operation of members of both the public and private sector who are dedicated to the conservation of our floral wealth. The publications committee that has motivated this series consists of the following bodies: The Branch of Forestry of the Department of Environment Affairs, the National Botanic Gardens of South Africa, the Department of Nature and Environmental Conservation of the Cape, the National Parks Board, the Bolus Herbarium of the University of Cape Town, the Botanical Research Institute of Stellenbosch and the Botanical Society of South Africa.

Special mention must be made of the financial contributions made by the Branch of Forestry of the Department of Environment Affairs, the Department of Nature and Environmental Conservation of the Cape, Endangered Wild Life Trust, the S.A. Nature Foundation and the Botanical Society of South Africa, which make it possible for these guides to be published and sold at a reasonable price. A particular word of thanks is hereby extended to members of the Cape Provincial Council for their generous contribution towards this series.

Acknowledgements

A book such as this cannot possibly be produced without the assistance of many people and we have indeed been fortunate that so many have been unsparing of their time, effort, advice and constructive criticism.

First and foremost we must thank Mrs. Kay Bergh, Chairman of the Publications Committee of the Botanical Society of South Africa. Hers has been the task of ironing out the innumerable problems associated with the production and publication of this Guide, acting as editor co-ordinator, mediator and Solomon. We wish to thank Mr. Wim Reynders for the time and effort spent designing this guide and for overseeing the actual production and Lt. Cdr. Geary-Cooke for his help in bringing the project to completion.

We are also most grateful to Dr. J.P. Rourke and the staff of the Compton Herbarium, Kirstenbosch, especially Mrs. Suzette Foster who with the aid of Mrs. Pat Morgan of the Botanical Society of South Africa, typed and corrected both the final English and Afrikaans texts at break-neck speed to meet the printers' deadline.

Our special thanks go to Mr. and Mrs. W.J. le Roux for translating the entire text into Afrikaans in the short period of a few weeks, Miss Annelise le Roux of the Department of Nature and Environmental Conservation of the Cape over five weekends edited the entire translation of the Afrikaans botanical text. We wish to thank her not only for this arduous task but for the many clarifications thereby incorporated in the English text.

Dr. P. Vorster of the University of Stellenbosch kindly translated the Glossary into Afrikaans.

Botanical experts from far and wide have assisted in identifying specimens and checking the accuracy of the text and we owe them an enormous debt of gratitude. They are in alphabetical order:

Dr. H. Baijnath; Miss W.F. Barker; Mr. Bruce Bayer; Dr. M. de Vos; Miss E. Esterhuysen; Mrs. P. Fairall; Dr. P. Goldblatt; Prof. A.V. Hall; Dr. O. Hillard; Dr. H.P. Linder; Dr. D. Koutnik; Mr. R.O. Moffett; Mrs. M. O'Connor Fenton; Mr. E.G.H. Oliver; Miss P. Perry; Dr. J.P. Rourke; Prof. E.A. Schelpe; Mrs. S. Schelpe; Miss D. Snijman; Mr. C. Stirton; Mr. J. Vlok; Dr. I. Williams.

We must also thank Mr. M. Viviers and Mr. G. Forsyth of the Branch of Forestry, Jonkershoek for assisting so enthusiastically; Mr. A. van der Zeyde, Curator of the Harold Porter Gardens, Betty's Bay, for his friendly courtesy, Dr. & Mrs. Ion Williams for many weekends spent at the White House whilst photographing at Hermanus and last but not least, Dr. Louis Vogelpoel and Prof. E.R. Orchard for finding and photographing the unusual *Mystropetalon polemanii* pictured in this Guide.

It has been most gratifying that Molteno Bros. and Oak Valley Estates from this area have supported the publication of this guide.

LEE BURMAN and ANNE BEAN

Foreword

The area covered by this wild flower guide has always been regarded as the showpiece of the fynbos. Here in the flower-laden Kogelberg and Hottentots Holland is the focal point of fynbos diversity — nowhere else is the flora more overpowering and one realises how intricate is the study and management of fynbos. A few thousand plant species grow here shoulder to shoulder — from the small Drosera species which must supplement their nutrition with protein to the magnificent marsh rose and the kloof forests. Here Williams Blake's words: "Everything that lives, lives not alone, nor for itself" truly obtain meaning.

The importance of the fynbos is stressed by the fact that three of the five guides produced so far cover the Cape Floral Kingdom. The Department, as the oldest conservation authority, is thankful for the contribution it could make towards this series as the education of the public is an important part of the successful conservation of this floral kingdom. Here, through the dedicated care of the Forestry Branch of the Department of Environment Affairs, species such as the marsh rose *(Orothamnus zeyheri)*, the blushing bride *(Serruria florida)*, the silver mimetes *(Mimetes argenteus)* and Stokoe's protea *(Protea stokoei)* and many other rare species have been saved from extinction. The research section of the Forestry Branch at Jonkershoek has for years done pioneer work in fynbos management.

The extensive Hottentots Holland Nature Reserve is regarded as one of the Forestry Branch's most important nature reserves and the future declaration of the Kogelberg as a wilderness area will further entrench the area for conservation. Declaration of the Hottentots Holland Mountain Catchment Area on private land not only simplified fire protection in the inaccessible areas, but also contributed towards keeping the area clean of invasive species.

The popular Hottentots Holland Hiking Trail and Grabouw Forest Hostel enable students and members of the public to form a deeper appreciation of the area.

The financial contribution of the Department of Environment Affairs towards the production of this guide, as well as others in the series, is tangible proof of its concern for this important educational project. We wish to express our deepest appreciation to Mr. & Mrs. Burman and Mrs. Anne Bean and other contributors to this guide.

We also wish to extend an invitation to the public, especially the young amongst us, to make extensive use of the hiking and nature trails in the area with a view to assisting us in the conservation task of this Department.

A. VAN DER DUSSEN
Deputy Director General: (Forestry)
Department of Environment Affairs
8 July 1985

Protea compacta

Introduction

The area of South Africa whose plants are illustrated in this guide is the richest floral area in Africa, and the heart of the fynbos — that unique, treeless, low shrubland of heaths, reeds and leathery-leaved proteas and their relations. Not only is the plant life incredibly rich; the scenery is also magnificent. From the restless Atlantic Ocean crashing against its southern shoreline, where the southern Right whale comes close inshore to calve each summer, to the highest peaks of the mountains which rise abruptly out of the sea to 1 300 m and extend north and east to Franschhoek, Jonkershoek, Groot Drakenstein, Hottentots Holland and the Klein River ranges, almost every step along the many hiking trails, or mile along the motorways, brings new and lovely vistas.

For the greater part of the year the climate is kind. Not quite hot enough, perhaps, for those used to the tropics, but almost never cold enough for frost either; the weather is usually a fine inducement to take a walk. When a cold front has deposited its snow on the high peaks, the extra nip in the air only adds zest to the beauty of the mountains.

The rain falls chiefly in the winter, so the hiker must be prepared with rainwear and jerseys. But in summer, when the grateful southeast tradewinds blanket the upper slopes in clouds of cooling mist, hikers can doff sunhats but need their jerseys and anoraks. Fortunate indeed are the lotus eaters within easy access of this shangri-la.

The major stresses challenging the vegetation throughout the fynbos region are the frequent strong winds accompanied by long periods without rain in the summer, but this area suffers least: proximity to the sea, reliable rainfall in winter and equally reliable cloud condensation in summer create bogs and seepages and keep the streams running all year.

GEOLOGY. The geology of the southwestern Cape is relatively uncomplicated. The basic ingredients consist of three different rock types. The foundation is of ancient Malmesbury shale, a compacted mud laid down under the sea before the dawn of life on earth. This foundation was subjected to tremendous pressure and upheaval due to massive invasion by molten granite from below. The mass was lifted above the sea and subjected to a period of erosion long enough to turn it into a flat-topped tableland. The whole area then sank once more beneath the sea, and into the depths were washed enormous volumes of sand from the adjacent land surfaces, to form the more than 3 000 m thickness of the Table Mountain series. Consolidation into a weather-resistant sandstone rock followed, and later the area was raised up once more to form the familiar coastline of the present. As it rose, many areas were subjected to folding and tilting creating the convoluted stratification seen in many areas today.

Running water finding its way down the interfaces crumbled by the process creates ravines; rain and wind remove loose surface particles to form the tow-

Yellow daisies at Jonkershoek

ering crags of the upper slopes, while the two zones of mud-stone sandwiched into the series form the gently sloping areas of the shalebands. The relatively high rainfall leaches out the minerals from this already mineral-poor soil, to create the thin coarse sands on which most of the fynbos plants now grow.

HABITATS. Plants are all more or less specialised in their growth requirements. As might be expected, all the major habitats carry their own characteristic vegetation. In this area, salt-marshes and estuaries, shifting dunes, sea-splashed rock cliffs, flat, often ill-drained coastal flats, river valleys, mountain slopes, crags and cloud zone all have their own distinctive assemblages; as do the granitic, shaly, sandy and rocky places.

In addition, the jumble of mountain ranges gives rise to a wealth of microhabitats each with its own angle relative to the sun, degree of shelter from the wind, moisture regime and altitude. Each provides a unique home to the liking of a select band of species found nowhere else. Therefore, in this marvellously diverse plant wonderland, every few strides reveal some plant not seen before. For those prepared to look with sharp eyes and a critical mind, these mountains offer a lifetime of new discoveries.

FIRE. Fire is one of the forces playing a particularly crucial role in shaping the fynbos. Fire is inevitable in the inflammable, often resinous vegetation. One spark in a strong southeaster during a dry period is enough to set a mountain ablaze. Old veld which has not seen a fire for a generation or more, although apparently quite destroyed, recovers like the phoenix from its ashes over a period of years. A multitude of geophytes not seen before the fire, burst suddenly into bloom, a few as soon as 3 weeks after a fire, a renaissance, rapid, unexpected and so beautiful that a walk in the wet season following a summer fire can be a breath-taking experience for the connoisseur. A wealth of orchids, *Iridaceae, Amaryllidaceae,* and *Liliaceae* will make their entrances and exits for the next few seasons before sinking back into the obscurity of sterile leafiness. Meanwhile, the protea flowerheads, having held their seeds in fireproof wraps until the parent plants succumbed to the flames, open, releasing a mass of seeds in readiness for the cool rains of autumn.

Half the fynbos plants are now believed to have adopted another strategy. Their seeds are provided with luscious waxy caps beloved by the large ants of the fynbos, and being thrown out as they ripen, the seeds land on the ground, whence they are feverishly garnered and taken below. There the ants eat off the caps and leave the seeds in the security of their deep passageways until the fire has passed. Then, by a trigger not yet understood, the seeds spring to life and produce a new generation of shrubs to replace the old.

Yet other species have developed stout woody underground stumps. After the fire has destroyed all aerial stems, only a brief period elapses before buds below ground produce a new crop of shoots from the old stumps.

Gradually all the plant species present before the fire are replaced by a new generation, and at the same time the mammals, reptiles, birds and amphibians, also disrupted by the passage of the fire, reappear, and the veld is as it was before. Such a process takes many years but as long as the next fire is delayed for a long period, and the fire occurs in summer, no harm is done.

Leucadendron gandogeri above Hermanus

Recent studies indicate that summer fires at 20 year intervals or longer do not damage the fynbos because the components have all had adequate time to make seed. Each species in the fynbos has its own rate of growing to reproductive maturity, some taking one season, others many years. But the more frequent the fires, the more species that do not have time to mature, and the greater the number of species that are exterminated. The drier the area, the more slowly all the species grow, and even 20 years may be too short an interval.

CONSERVATION. The bulk of the area dealt with in this guide is too steep for exploitation by man, the chief destroyer of natural beauty. Much of the area is fortunately officially protected by the status of mountain catchment areas and nature reserves. But looking into the future the picture is sombre. There is a tendency to regard nature reserves as 'places held temporarily until someone discovers another better use for them' which must be resisted unceasingly by society.

There are many other matters of concern. Flat areas on mountains and coastal plains are already largely transformed beyond recovery by afforestation, agriculture or urban sprawl. Some species whose special habitats these were

Springflowers at Vermont, near Hermanus

have been eradicated or are fast disappearing, *Leucadendron globosum, Mimetes hirtus, M. stokoei* and *Witsenia maura* to mention just a few. Many more are threatened. The survival of the veld is also imperilled by invasions of alien weeds, a host of them imported from other lands. Many are to be found in this area. Wattles planted to stabilise naturally loose dunes made more loose by overgrazing are spreading fast into the adjacent veld. The wattles catch windblown sand, adding progressively to the steepness of the beach until it no longer can support the erstwhile abundant white mussels of the shoreline. Australian myrtle, planted as hedgerows now run amuck in the deep coastal sands. The bugtree is spread by birds deep into forest glades. Sesbania, that pernicious orange beauty resistant to wind, sand and drought yet liking our river courses so much that it threatens to supplant our natural riverine plants. Hakea and pine whose seeds are blown from the infestations allowed to develop by some landowners adjoining the pristine veld, necessitating constant vigilant eradication programmes by reserve management. A new threat is posed by *Acacia elata*, a popular fast-growing shelter tree whose invasive seedlings are giving ample warning that they should be removed from the area. All are present and contribute their share to the stresses being borne by vegetation already under siege from too frequent veld fires or fires lit out of season, by picking, by trail bikes and by careless hikers. Only heightened awareness and increased help by all of us who care for the veld will ensure the long-term survival of this superb natural heritage.

Help can take many forms. Join conservation groups such as the Botanical Society or the Wildlife Society; join hack groups or get to know the pest plants and pull them out wherever you find them. Please mind your veld manners: help to prevent erosion by keeping to the paths; be careful not to cause veldfires. Avoid planting pest plants in your garden because their seeds are a source of infestation in the veld.

HOW TO USE THIS GUIDE TO NAME A PLANT. With the plant in front of you, look at the illustrations and then read the text, noting the special features. Check flowering time and habitat. If all match, the name can with some reliability be awarded to the plant. Do not try to remember the plant and name it at home, — this is a fairly sure recipe for error.

Almost all the features used in this guide are visible to the eye, and have been selected with a view to being available on a living plant in situ. The enthusiast may find a x10 magnifying glass an additional aid to accuracy. Hair and gland characters are most visible if the object is held up to the light. Anthers are best seen in a very newly opened bud. The seeds and ovary are clearest in maturing flowers after the petals have withered. A glossary is provided to help with the few technical terms which have proved unavoidable.

Do not expect to be able to name every plant you see. Plants vary. Although a few thousand species are found in this area, only a fraction of the species present could be illustrated. While it will be possible to identify plants in many instances even as far away as the Cedarberg, the species composition of the veld changes dramatically once out of the moist coastal strip and high mountains and onto the clay soils of the inland areas which have not been included in this guide.

THE HIKING TRAILS. The plants illustrated here have all been seen alongside public paths and roads, and were chosen because they were common or striking or important in the area. They may occur elsewhere.

Before describing the hiking trails in more detail, a word of warning about the perils of the Boland trail is necessary. This area is subject to quite sudden and savage changes of weather especially in the cooler months. It is essential to carry warm and rainproof clothing irrespective of the weather at the outset of a hike. Rain accompanied by near freezing temperatures and strong winds rapidly reduces body temperature to dangerously low levels, and several hikers have died of exposure through being unprepared.

THE BOLAND TRAIL This is a composite trail under the management of the National Hiking Way Board taking three days from west to east, and two days from south to north. This book applies to the whole trail, and for anyone interested in identifying flowers on the Boland Trail this guide is essential.

However, if you want to see flowers you do not have to hump a heavy pack for days, since the Boland Trail breaks down easily into a series of relatively short walks starting from different points. Permits are obtainable from the Branch of Forestry, Private Bag 9005, Cape Town.

The Walks

1. SIR LOWRY'S PASS
This is the original starting point of the Boland Trail, which takes off from a parking place on the eastern side of the N2 at the summit of Sir Lowry's Pass. For the first kilometre the trail skirts the peaks looking down on the Grabouw pine plantation. There is a wide variety of plants including *Protea neriifolia*, *Gladiolius blommesteinii*, *Erodium incarnatum*, and *Erica massonii*.

Soon the path leaves the contour, does a short detour up the old Hottentots Holland Kloof (where the old pass runs), then crosses a plateau and zig-zags onto a higher level. There are fascinating views of False Bay. The path runs below Verkykerskop and seven kilometres from Sir Lowry's Pass emerges onto a tarred road. Turn right and follow this road.

In the little valleys on the left are magnificent *Retzia capensis* as well as *Raspalia microphylla* and *Hypocalyptus coluteoides*. The tarred road leads down to a plantation where you turn right onto a dirt road which eventually links back to the Sir Lowry's Pass path. You will find both *Erica nana* and *Erica banksia* growing on the rocks.

2. NUWEBERG
Situated near the top of Viljoenspas, this forestry station is reached from the National Road by turning off at Elgin. From it begins the south-north part of the Boland Trail, a path passing through the plantations and then over a nek 3,5 kilometres from Nuweberg. The bright pink *Erica tegulaefolia* is plentiful on the slope, with the uncommon *Stilbe mucronata* on the rocky hilltops. The road forks, the left leading to Landdroskop (the main hut on the trail), whilst to the right it leads to Franschhoek.

Follow the trail to the right and you will cross the headwaters of the Riviersonderend. Here you will see some magnificent *Senecio coleophyllus*, a tall mauve daisy. The path turns up Boegoe Kloof, and after a while the Trail leaves Boegoe Kloof heading eastward. Your walk, however, continues up Boegoe Kloof into a really wild mountain glen.

Psoraleas and everlastings grow in profusion, dominated in places by huge *Protea cynaroides* and quantities of the rather uncommon and attractive *Dilatris viscosa* (bloedwortel).

There is a little waterfall and rapid where you can lunch before returning to Nuweberg.

3. JAN JOUBERTS GAT

Jan Jouberts Gat is the first really big kloof reached when you ascend Franschhoek Pass from the Villiersdorp side. Park your car next to the bridge and follow the little path which rises up the left (southern) side of the kloof, to join the Boland Trail about an hour from the road. Turn right along the Trail and it will take you across the Jan Jouberts River and onto the plateau called laaste-vlakte. If you continue along this path it will take you down the old road Simon van der Stel called the "Olifanten Pad" to join the Franschhoek Pass just above the town. Alternatively take the jeep-track you reach 15 minutes after crossing the river and follow it to the right; it will lead you down in wide loops to the Franschhoek Pass, less than half-an-hour from Jan Jouberts Gat.

Apart from the variety of flowers you will undoubtedly see, the top of the Jan Jouberts Gat pass is the only place in this area where we have found *Oldenbergia paradoxa* growing among the rocks. You may find fields of *Ursinia paleacea* and the occasional *Edmondia pinifolia*.

4. JONKERSHOEK

The south to north route over the Boland Trail ends at Jonkershoek, but you can reach that beautiful valley easily by driving through Stellenbosch. If you get a forestry permit you can even drive into the reserve and park at the far end, where the road turns back towards the Forestry Station.

There are two walking routes at the far end of the valley: the one follows the Eersterivier up the valley to Tweedewaterval, whilst the second starts up a little firebreak on the east of the road and leads up the slope to the Ridge Peak. Eventually you can follow this route in a wide circuit along the peaks to join Boschkloof, and descend via the Boland Trail, or take the extremely steep shortcut down the river kloof called the "Kurktrekker".

The interesting thing about Jonkershoek is that, although part of the Hottentots Holland, its vegetation differs sharply from the rest of the Trail, since granite is the predominant soil here. You will therefore find the following growing at Jonkershoek: *Erica grandiflora, Halleria eliptica, Leucospermum gueinzii, Leucospermum lineare, Lichtensteinia lacera, Phylica pubescens, Protea burchellii, Pteronia camphorata.*

5. KLEINMOND

There are three different walks at Kleinmond: the first is a high-level climb which starts on Jean's Hill, above 16th Street Kleinmond, and follows the crest of the ridge over the Three Sisters and down through the Kleinmond Nature Reserve to Fairy Glen. Unless you are very fit and very keen I would advise amateur botanists to leave this route alone. Instead take:

(a) **The Nature Trail** which leaves the Jean's Hill path halfway up the slope and contours below Sandown Peak and the Three Sisters. It reaches an old quarry and then, keeping to the south of the stream, descends to Fairy

Following page: A colourful scene at Jonkershoek

Glen. If, however, you wish to see the superb Kleinmond Nature Reserve you can cross the old quarry and follow the wide firebreak across the plateau until it reaches the path from the Three Sisters. If you turn right you can climb all the way up to the top of the reserve, which in summer is covered with the very local yellow *Erica tenax*. On the peaks you will find *Nivenia levynsiae*, with *Brunia stokoei* and the more common *Nivenia stokoei* on the lower slopes.

(b) **Palmietstrand:** From Fairy Glen you can return to Kleinmond by another route, the Palmietstrand. If you cross the road at Fairy Glen and descend to the Palmiet lagoon you can follow the trail along the edge of the lagoon and back along the seashore to Kleinmond, a pleasant varied walk. There are numerous flowers to see, amongst them: *Zaluzianskya capensis*, *Phylica ericoides*, various Rhus species and, at the lagoon edge, a magnificent *Podocarpus latifolius*.

6. **BETTY'S BAY**

Betty's Bay lies at the southern foot of the Hottentots Holland. The slopes high above are out of bounds to walkers as they form part of the Kogelberg Reserve which is closed to the public. The bay's claim to botanic distinction is the Harold Porter Botanic Reserve one of the Kirstenbosch series of National Botanic Gardens. Apart from what you can find in the reserve there are two walks that repay doing. The first is:

(a) **Luiperdskloof,** reached through a locked gate at the top of the garden (the key is held by the curator). The path climbs a kloof filled with indigenous trees and vegetation to a series of waterfalls, where you can find *Disa uniflora*. The second is

(b) **Rod's Trail** which starts from the Harold Porter Botanic Reserve and leads past Disakloof and along the slopes of the Voorberg for an hour, descending near the cafe. Here you can cross the road to reach the seashore along which you can return to your starting-point. Surprisingly enough there are plenty of flowers on the shoreline too. There are a number of interesting flowers to be seen at Betty's Bay, including *Mimetes hirtus*, *Erica patersonii*, *Erica retorta*, *Satyrium carneum*, *Leucospermum oleifolium*, *Brunia albiflora*, and *Olea exasperata*.

7. **HERMANUS**

The Kleinrivier mountains, and their slopes leading down to the sea, on which Hermanus sprawls, is one of the richest floral areas of mountain fynbos.

(a) **Fernkloof Reserve** is the pride of Hermanus and the heart of environmental activity, supported by the strong Hermanus Botanical Society. There are over 40 kilometres of paths in this reserve covering a large part of the Kleinrivier mountains. Most of these paths start at the kiosk in the reserve, and there is a map of the paths which is obtainable at Hermanus. In addition you can drive into the flower area by following Rotary Drive which starts just at the entrance of the town and traverses the mountains above providing fantastic scenic viewpoints.

Amongst the multitude of flowers to be seen in Fernkloof are *Adenandra brachyphylla, Aulax umbellata, Erica aristata, Erica cumuliflora, Erica irbyana, Gladiolus bullatus, Gladiolus debilis, Hermas villosa, Lachenalia pearsii* (on the lower slopes), *Leucadendron gandogeri, Protea compacta, Protea longifolia* and *Sonderothamnus speciosus.*

(b) **Cliff Path.** In addition to the mountain slopes of Fernkloof there are two long walks along the Cliff Path through the thick vegetation which covers the rocky cliffs above the sea. This area is also very rich in flowers, and the following are amongst those found there: *Bonatea speciosa, Carpobrotus edulis, Cotyledon orbiculata, Ferraria crispa, Frankenia pulverulenta, Geissorhiza aspera* (which forms a carpet in spring), *Gladiolus carmineus* (cliff lily), *Haemanthus coccineus, Lachenalia rubida, Limonium scabrum, Orpheum frutescens, Polygala myrtifolia.*

(c) **Vermont.** The vegetation on the beachfront at Vermont, near Hermanus, is the home of a number of flowers typical of the sand dunes as opposed to the rocks of the Cliff Path. Included are *Anomalesia cunonia, Heliophila linearis, Manulea tomentosa, Sutera tristis* and *Zaluzianskya villosa.*

These are the principal walks along which you will see the flowers of the mountain fynbos, and we are sure you will enjoy them all.

Further information

Contact the following organisations:

The Botanical Society of South Africa
Kirstenbosch, Claremont 7735.
Tel: (021) 771725

The National Botanic Gardens
of South Africa
Kirstenbosch, Claremont 7735
Tel: (021) 771166

The Department of Nature
and Environmental Conservation
Private Bag 9086, Cape Town 8000
Tel: (021) 450227

The Branch of Forestry
Private Bag 9005, Cape Town 8000
Tel: (021) 467010

APONOGETONACEAE

Aponogeton distachyos Wateruintjie Waterblommetjie
A tuberous-rooted aquatic perennial with floating leaves 60-200 mm long, borne on stalks. It has an edible, sweetly scented, forked flowerhead, used to make the local dish "waterblommetjie bredie". It is found in dense colonies in ponds, ditches and deep sluggish streams from Nieuwoudtville to Knysna. (July-Dec)
 About 30 species occur in Africa, Madagascar, Asia and Australia of which there are 5 in South Africa, but only 1 in this area.

POACEAE

Pseudopentameris brachyphylla
A perennial grass forming stout tufts to 1 m tall with cylindrical, hollow, densely-leafed stems. As in all grasses the lower part of the leaf sheaths the stem, and the upper part is free and usually flattened. Where 2 halves join there is a ligule which can be a thin collar, a heavy rim, or, as in this species, a hairy fringe. The wind-pollinated flowers with freely projecting stigmas and stamens are grouped into purple and pale yellow flowerheads called spikelets. Occasional on mountain slopes from Caledon to Swellendam. (Oct)
 There are 2 species confined to the southwestern Cape.

CYPERACEAE

Mariscus thunbergii
A robust tufted perennial to 1 m tall with a stiff 3-sided solid stem and basal leaves slightly shorter than the stem. The stalks of the flower spikes are of unequal length and the flower clusters are surrounded by a number of bristly, leafy bracts. Occurring in damp places or forest verges along the coastal belt from Clanwilliam to Natal. (June-Dec)
 There are about 200 species world-wide in warm moist areas, of which about 4 occur in the Cape.

Tetraria thermalis Bergpalmiet
An exceptionally coarse, tufted plant to 2,5 m high, with flat, swordlike leaves, to 20 mm broad, having a sharp cutting edge. The 3-sided solid flowering stems are longer than the leaves. The flowers are clustered within large brown overlapping bracts. Widespread on flats and mountain slopes from the Peninsula to Riversdale. It is one of the first plants to resprout after fire. (June-Oct)
 There are about 40 species in Africa and Australia, of which about 14 occur in this area.

Aponogeton distachyos

Pseudopentameris brachyphylla

Mariscus thunbergii

Tetraria thermalis

RESTIONACEAE

These are rush-like plants which have unisexual flowers borne on separate, often dissimilar plants which can often be matched by comparing the sheaths on the stems. The flowers are grouped together in spikelets, usually in the axils of dry, papery bracts. The leaves are dry sheaths which are split to the base and often drop off early. They take the place of grasses in the fynbos.

Elegia persistens (male)
Plants forming loose tussocks about 500 mm tall. The flowering stems are unbranched but it may have occasional weaker, branched sterile stems. The leaf-sheaths fall off early. Conspicuous spreading brown papery spathes expose large clusters of male flowers. Often frequent in gravelly soils on mid or lower slopes.
   There are 35 species confined to the fynbos areas of the Cape, with 23 being recorded from this area.

Elegia persistens (female)
The female of this species differs from the male in having a narrowly cylindrical inflorescence completely hidden within the pale brown overlapping spathes, 20-30 mm long.

Elegia filacea (male)
Plants forming small tussocks, less than 500 mm tall. The stems are slender, unbranched, and lose their sheathing leaves early. The inflorescence is about 20 mm long, with spathes 10 mm long. It is very common on sandy flats at most altitudes.

Elegia filacea (female)
Rather similar to the male, but with the flowers more or less obscured by the spathes.

Elegia persistens (male)   *Elegia persistens (female)*

Elegia filacea (male)   *Elegia filacea (female)*

RESTIONACEAE

Ceratocaryum argenteum (female)
Plants forming large tussocks, to 2,5 m tall, with unbranched stems about 6 mm in diameter. The inflorescence consists of 3-8 densely packed spikelets within a shiny brown bony spathe 40-60 mm long. Each spikelet has only a single flower with 2 styles, enclosed by numerous slender pale brown papery bracts about 20 mm long. It is found in dense stands in damp seepages at lower altitudes.

There are 5 species confined to the fynbos areas of the Cape, with 2 from this area.

Ceratocaryum argenteum (male)
Similar in size to the female plant, the male has an inflorescence with spathes which soon drop off, exposing very large numbers of 5 mm long papery flowers.

Elegia capensis
Plants forming large tussocks, to 2,5 m tall. The stems have whorls of numerous slender sterile branches at the nodes. Male and female inflorescences are similar, with spathes which soon drop off. It is common along streams and wet seepages and it may form large dense stands.

The only other species with clusters of sterile branches at the nodes, *E. equisetacea,* can be distinguished by having spathes which do not drop off.

Cannomois virgata (male)
Plants forming tussocks 1-2,5 m tall, the stems having numerous branches. The inflorescence is up to 300 mm long and consists of large numbers of many-flowered brown spikelets, each 5-10 mm long. The female plants usually have solitary spikelets which are spindle-shaped and 20-50 mm long. Frequent along streams and in wet seepages.

There are 6 species, largely confined to the fynbos areas of the Cape, with a further 2 being recorded from this area, both with simple unbranched stems.

Ceratocaryum argenteum (female)

Ceratocaryum argenteum (male)

Elegia capensis

Cannomois virgata (male)

COMMELINACEAE

Commelina africana   Wandering Jew   Wandelende Jood
A weak prostrate perennial with well-defined nodes and leaves 30-50 mm long by 10-15 mm wide. Common on lower slopes or near streams from the Cape Peninsula eastward to Natal, and throughout the tropics of the Old World. (Nov-June)

There are about 230 species worldwide, of which 12 occur in South Africa, but only 1 occurs wild in this area. The pretty blue *C. benghalensis* of suburban gardens is an introduced weed of cultivation.

LILIACEAE

Chlorophytum rigidum   *ASPHODELACEAE**
A tufted perennial with stiff, smooth, narrow leaves approximately 300 mm long by 8 mm broad, much shorter than the branched flowering stem. The flowers, 25-35 mm across, emerge singly from a cluster of small, dark bracts with tissue-like edges and have white tepals with a brown midline. Recorded from stony ground at mid-altitudes in the west of this area northwards to Worcester. (May-Oct)

There are about 90 species, mainly in tropical Africa and Asia, of which 1 other may occur in this area: *C. undulatum*, with an unbranched or only 2-branched stem, has entirely tissuelike bracts and red-striped tepals.

Agapanthus africanus   *ALLIACEAE**   Bloulelie
An evergreen perennial with numerous thick strap-shaped leaves 100-250 mm long and 9-12 mm broad with mucilaginous sap. The 12-30 trumpet-shaped flowers, 25-40 mm long, are borne in a large head at the end of an unbranched stem. Common, especially in rocky places on mountains, it occurs from the Cape Peninsula to Swellendam and blooms profusely after veld fires. (Dec-Apr)

There are 10 species in the moister parts of South Africa, of which there is 1 other in this area: *A. walshii* of the Steenbras mountains is distinguished by its tubular flowers.

Albuca canadensis   *HYACINTHACEAE**   Soldier-in-a-box
                                                                      Geldbeursie
A bulbous geophyte with 3-6 broad, soft, basal sheathing leaves 200-600 mm long by 10-30 mm broad, withering at flowering-time. The unbranched flowering stem, 250-900 mm long bears flowers 20-25 mm long with spreading outer lobes. The inner lobes form a tube around the 3 fertile and 3 sterile stamens. Occurring in sandy places on flats and lower slopes from Clanwilliam to the Hermanus area. (Sept-Nov)

There are about 30 species in Africa, of which 3 occur in this area. *A. fragrans* has a faintly sweet scent and 6 fertile stamens; whilst *A cooperi* has the old leaves forming a fibrous wrapping around the bulb.

*See page 210

Commelina africana

Chlorophytum rigidum

Agapanthus africanus

Albuca canadensis

LILIACEAE

Bulbine lagopus   *ASPHODELACEAE**
A tuberous-rooted perennial with a clump of semi-cylindrical, 300 mm by 12 mm leaves from the base. The unbranched flowering stem grows to 600 mm and bears flowers 6-9 mm in diameter with bearded stamens, emerging from papery bracts with jagged edges. Recorded at lower altitudes and near the sea from the Cape Peninsula to Port Elizabeth and beyond. (Sept-Dec)

There are about 50 species in Africa, of which about 4 occur in this area. The similar yellow or white-flowered *B. frutescens* which also flowers in spring, has a branched stem which bears some leaves. Two other species flower in the autumn.

Bulbinella triquetra   *ASPHODELACEAE**   Katstert
A tuberous-rooted perennial 150-450 mm tall, with a clump of threadlike leaves 100-250 mm long and a dainty head of white flowers on an unbranched stem. The bright yellow stamens lack the beards of the otherwise similar bulbine. Occurring in sandy soil from Malmesbury to Bredasdorp. (Mainly Feb-May)

There are about 19 species in South Africa and New Zealand, of which some 12 occur in the Cape, and 3 in this area, the others blooming in the spring: the bright yellow-flowered *B. floribunda* and a cream-coloured unnamed species.

Drimia media   *HYACINTHACEAE**   Jeukbol
A geophyte with a huge bulb and 8-10 half-cylindrical, rigid leaves 100-250 mm long. The unbranched flowering stem is about twice this height, bearing 12 mm long flowers on short stalks. The tepals are silvery within and brownish on the outside and reflex sharply backwards. Recorded in sandy soils from Saldanha Bay to Knysna, it blooms most abundantly after veld fires. (Jan-Mar)

There are about 25 species in South Africa of which 3 occur in this area. The other 2 are leafless at flowering time. *D. elata*, 500-900 mm tall, has flowers 15 mm long on stalks only a little shorter than the flowers, and *D. forsteri*, the 'maerman', is 1-2 m tall with many crowded flowers on very short stalks.

Onixotis punctata   *COLCHICACEAE**   Hanekammetjie
A cormous, usually 3-leaved geophyte with flat leaves 60-100 mm long and 4-6 mm wide, 2 at ground level and 1 raised up on the stem. It bears 5-20 white or maroon flowers, with or without pink spots, on a stem up to 300 mm tall. Recorded on flats and slopes from Ceres to Swellendam, in greatest abundance after veld-fires. (July-Sept)

There are 2 species, the other being the marsh-loving *O. triquetra* with 3-sided leaves.

*See page 210

Bulbine lagopus

Bulbinella triquetra

Drimia media

Onixotis punctata

LILIACEAE

Lachenalia orchioides   *HYACINTHACEAE**   Wild hyacinth
Blouviooltjie
A bulbous geophyte 120-250 mm tall. Its usually spotted stem bears 2 erect leaves up to 25 mm wide. The cream to yellow-green or blue-purple, sessile flowers are sweetly-scented and borne in a crowded head, the tepals concealing the stamens and style. Occurring on a variety of soils from the Cedarberg to the Cape Peninsula and on to the Gourits River. (June-Sept)

There are 85 species distributed throughout the Cape Province, the southern Orange Free State and Namibia, of which 11 occur in this area. The similarly coloured *L. fistulosa* is the only other species in this area with sessile flowers, but these are bell-shaped and face outwards.

Lachenalia peersii   *HYACINTHACEAE**   Bekkies
A bulbous geophyte, to 350 mm tall, with 1 or 2 leaves up to 20 mm wide and often tinged maroon below. The carnation-scented bell-shaped 7-10 mm long flowers are white with pink tips fading deeper pink. The outer tepals are slightly shorter than the inner ones and often green-tipped. It is common on rocky flats and slopes from Cape Hangklip to Hermanus. (Oct-Nov)

It may be confused with *L. rosea* which has 1 strap-shaped leaf and stamens visible at the mouth of the flower.

Lachenalia rubida   *HYACINTHACEAE**   Bergnaeltjie
Sandkalossie
A bulbous geophyte, to 150 mm tall, clasped at the base by 1 or 2, 150 mm by 25 mm leaves which are often broadest in the upper half, but taper abruptly into a V-shaped tip. The short-stalked, cylindrical, slightly drooping 30 mm long flowers are coral to red with purple tips, and grouped 6-20 together. The style eventually projects. Occurring on sandy soils from Lamberts Bay to the Cape Peninsula and east to George. (Apr-July)

The very similar *L. bulbifera* flowers slightly later and has a single, broader, usually unspotted leaf.

Wurmbea spicata   *COLCHICACEAE**   Kaffertjie
A cormous geophyte with 3 channelled, basal leaves up to 200 mm long. The unbranched, 50-200 mm long flowering stem bears a spike of almost sessile flowers, with the tepals joined into a tube below. It has a 3-forked style, and 6 stamens attached high up on the tepals in association with raised, fleshy, nectar glands. The corm is said to be poisonous, and the flowers are wonderfully scented in the evening. It occurs from the Gifberg and Nieuwoudtville to the Cape Peninsula and on to Swellendam. (Aug-Nov)

There are about 37 species in Africa and Australia of which some 5 occur in this area.

*See page 210

Lachenalia orchioides

Lachenalia peersii

Lachenalia rubida

Wurmbea spicata

LILIACEAE

Trachyandra hirsutiflora *ASPHODELACEAE**
A harshly hairy perennial with narrow leaves up to 600 mm long and 2 mm wide and an unbranched flowering stem shorter than the leaves. The densely-hairy flowers 12 mm long are followed by very hairy, oval, erect pods. Occurring on sandy or rocky flats from Clanwilliam to Caledon. (June-Dec)
   There are about 50 species in Africa, of which 46 occur in South Africa and 10 in this area.

Trachyandra hirsuta *ASPHODELACEAE**
A perennial with a fan of stiff, hairy, flat leaves 70-400 mm long and 5-20 mm wide, and a branched flowering stem to 600 mm. The hairless flowers are 10-12 mm long. It occurs on lower mountain slopes or flats, sometimes in marshes, from Piketberg to the Cape Peninsula and Caledon. (Sept-Oct)

Ornithogalum thyrsoides *HYACINTHACEAE** Chincherinchee
Tjienkerientjee
A bulbous geophyte with up to 7 basal leaves 150-300 mm long. The flowering stems grow to about 500 mm, and bear a variable number of white flowers, with or without a dark eye, which rise from broad papery bracts. This species is commercially valuable in the export cut-flower trade because of its long-lasting qualities, but is extremely poisonous to livestock. Recorded on lower slopes and sand flats from Namaqualand to Caledon, sometimes in large colonies. (Oct-Dec)
   There are about 120 species in Africa and Eurasia, of which 8 occur in this area. There are 5 other white-flowered species, including the broad-leafed *O. esterhuyseniae* of high altitudes in the Hottentots Holland mountains, *O. hispidum*, with hairy, threadlike leaves, and the widespread *O. juncifolium* which has smaller flowers.

Ornithogalum dubium *HYACINTHACEAE** Yellow chincherinchee
Geel Tjienkerientjee
A bulbous geophyte 100-500 mm high with hairy-edged, 50-200 mm by 5-30 mm leaves which appear before the flowers but often wither as they open. The 10-20 flowers may be orange or white, and are 10-20 mm long, with a dark-coloured, very short style. A variable, widespread, and locally common plant of rocky slopes, stony clay, or sandy flats from Clanwilliam to Paarl, and Caledon to Port Elizabeth and the eastern Cape. (Aug-Dec)
   O. graminifolium, with dull yellow or pink flowers, and 2-5 grasslike leaves to 250 mm long which dry to form a brittle thin neck, occurs on moist mountain slopes.

*See page 210

Trachyandra hirsutiflora   *Trachyandra hirsuta*

Ornithogalum thyrsoides   *Ornithogalum dubium*

LILIACEAE

Protasparagus aethiopicus *ASPARAGACEAE** Haakdoring
A variable plant which may be a woody climber to 7 m, or an erect shrub to 1 m. It has narrow flat leaves in groups of 3-6 or more, each leaf 10-40 mm by 1-2 mm. Spines are present on all nodes, except sometimes on those on the flowering stems. The very sweetly scented flowers, some 7 mm across, are borne in 30-50 mm long racemes and give rise to red berries. Occurring in coastal forest from the Cape Peninsula to the eastern Cape. (Jan-June)

There are about 80 species in Africa and Asia, of which 5 are recorded in this area. None of these has flattened leaves nor flowers in racemes.

Protasparagus rubicundus *ASPARAGACEAE** Wild asparagus
Wilde aspersie
A fibrous-rooted, hairless shrub with smooth, dark stems which can grow to 1,5 m in height, especially in shade. Sharp, slightly curving spines to 6 mm long occur on all but the flowering branches. The 6 mm long flowers, usually solitary in the axils of the 3-20 mm long needlelike leaves, give rise to red berries. Widespread from Clanwilliam to Uitenhage. (Jan-June)

Three other species in this area have similarly arranged flowers and needlelike leaves.

HAEMODORACEAE

Wachendorfia thyrsiflora
A perennial with reddish tuberous roots, growing to over 1 m in height, with a fan of hairless, pleated leaves 600-900 mm long and 5-9 mm wide. The bright golden hairy flowers are borne in clusters on delicate side shoots of a thick hairy, unbranched stem. Recorded in marshes from the Cape Peninsula to Port Elizabeth, often in dense stands. (Sept-Dec)

Wachendorfia paniculata Rooikanol Spinnekopblom
A slender perennial, more or less hairy, to 700 mm high, with reddish, tuberous roots and a fan of pleated leaves up to 400 mm long. The yellow flowers, up to 25 mm long, with the stamens almost as long, often have dark markings. Recorded in well-drained sands and coarse gravels from Clanwilliam to Port Elizabeth. (Sept-Oct)

There are 5 species endemic to the fynbos, of which 4 occur in this area. The other 2 species have apricot-coloured flowers. *W. brachyandra* has stamens much shorter than the tepals and grows in moist places, while *W. graminifolia* has stamens almost as long as the tepals and grows in drier places.

*See page 210

Protasparagus aethiopicus

Protasparagus rubicundus

Wachendorfia thyrsiflora

Wachendorfia paniculata

HAEMODORACEAE

Dilatris viscosa
A perennial to 600 mm tall with a fan of hairless leaves, much shorter than the flowering stem. The sticky, hairy, orange flowers are arranged in a rounded head, which can be 100 mm wide, each flower being about 13 mm long. Recorded from swamps or high mountain slopes in the summer cloud belt from Ceres to Riversdale. (Aug-Dec)

Dilatris pillansii   Rooiwortel
A perennial with bright red basal parts and a fan of stiff leaves up to 300 mm long and 3-5 mm broad. The softly-hairy flowers have round-tipped tepals up to 10 mm long and about 6 mm broad. The stamens are well inside the tepals. Recorded from the Cedarberg to Worcester and Bredasdorp, it blooms profusely after fires. (Aug-Jan)

There are 4 species endemic to the southwestern Cape, of which 3 occur in this area: the very similar *D. corymbosa* has pointed tepals, 2 of the stamens projecting beyond them.

Lanaria lanata   Cape edelweiss   Kapokblom
                                                                                               Perdekapok
A perennial to 800 mm with a rosette of stiff, narrow leaves, from a fire-resistant rootstock, and a dense woolly white head of mauve flowers (here seen in bud). Common and widespread on mountain slopes from Caledon to Port Elizabeth. It is not conspicuous except after a veld-fire, when it blooms early and profusely. (Nov-Jan)

There is only 1 species.

AMARYLLIDACEAE

Cyrtanthus leucanthus   Witbergpypie
A bulbous geophyte with flowering stem up to 250 mm long, bearing up to 3 flowers, each 40 mm long. The leaves are ⅔ as long as the stem and 1 mm wide, appearing after the flowers are over. It seldom flowers except in the first season after a veld fire, and occurs on sandy and rocky flats in the Caledon district. (Jan-Mar)

There are about 50 species in Africa, most of which occur in southern Africa and four in this area. This is the only cream-flowered species. The others are: the magnificent *C. carneus*, up to 1 m tall, with large soft pink to crimson flowers up to 75 mm long, and long strap-shaped leaves; the red-flowered *C. angustifolius* with drooping 40-50 mm long flowers, yellow in the throat; and *C. ventricosus* which bears its dainty red flowers on a 100-200 mm tall stalk.

Dilatris viscosa

Dilatris pillansii

Lanaria lanata

Cyrtanthus leucanthus

AMARYLLIDACEAE

Brunsvigia marginata
A bulbous geophyte, leafless at flowering time, with flattened stems to 200 mm tall. They bear 10-30 bright red flowers, each about 25 mm long, in a compact head. The 4 or more spreading tongue-shaped leaves are 150-220 mm long and 50-70 mm broad. Occurring on the upper mountain slopes from Tulbagh and Ceres to Franschhoek, it flowers most abundantly after veld fires. (Mar-July)

There are about 20 species, mostly South African, of which 2 occur in this area.

Brunsvigia orientalis   Candelabra flower   Koningskandelaar
                                                       Perdespookbossie
A bulbous geophyte up to 500 mm tall bearing a head of many short-lived flowers 50-60 mm long with the lobes turning back in the upper half. They are followed by the familiar fruiting heads which roll about in the wind, scattering the seeds as they rotate. After flowering about 4 tongue-shaped, closely-ribbed leaves 150-225 mm by 75-125 mm appear and spread out along the ground. It is locally common on sandy flats on the coastal plains between Saldanha Bay and Knysna. (Feb-Apr)

Nerine sarniensis   Guernsey Lily   Berglelie
A bulbous geophyte, with about 6 strap-shaped leaves 250-450 mm long and 12-28 mm broad, produced after the flowers. These flowers are bright scarlet (occasionally pink) and gold-dusted, about 40 mm long, and borne on slightly flattened stalks. The colour of the bracts matches that of the flowers. It occurs on rocky mountain slopes from Clanwilliam to Caledon. (Mar-May)

There are about 30 species widespread in South Africa, with innumerable garden hybrids, but there is only 1 other species in this area; *N. humilis*, which has pink or rosy flowers with green bracts, the stamens and style curving to one side. The leaves are contemporary with the flowers.

Haemanthus coccineus   April Fool   Blood Flower
                                                           Bergajuin
A bulbous geophyte with speckled and barred flowering stem 60-200 mm long followed by 2 leathery, smooth, tongue-shaped leaves 25-210 mm wide, curving out and downwards. It occurs in forest, scrub and open veld from sea level on the beach to the lower mountain slopes, from Namaqualand to the eastern Cape. (Dec-Apr)

There are about 90 species, mainly in Africa, of which 45 occur in southern Africa, and 3 in this area. *H. sanguineus* (=*H. rotundifolius*) has broad rough-textured, unspeckled leaves pressed flat to the ground; and the very local, brilliant red to pink *H. canaliculatus* with smooth leaves less than 30 mm wide, deeply channelled above, is confined to marshes in the southwest of this area.

Brunsvigia marginata *Brunsvigia orientalis*

Nerine sarniensis *Haemanthus coccineus*

AMARYLLIDACEAE

Amaryllis belladonna   March lily   Belladonna lily
                                                     Maartblom

A bulbous geophyte with a leafless flowering stem 400-900 mm long, bearing 2-10 trumpet-shaped, heavily-scented flowers in various shades of pink. There are 6-10 strap-shaped floppy leaves 200-600 mm long and 20-40 mm wide, produced after the flowers. Occurring at lower altitudes on slopes of mountains and hills, it blooms as the vernacular name suggests, in autumn, especially after veld fires. (Feb-Apr)

There is only 1 species, confined to the southwest Cape.

HYPOXIDACEAE

Spiloxene capensis   Peacock flower   Poublommetjie
                                                        Sterretjie

A very variable cormous geophyte whose 4-12 leaves are Y-shaped in cross-section in the upper half. The solitary yellow, pink or white flowers on hollow stalks are enormously variable in size from 15-100 mm across, with or without an iridescent dark centre. It occurs in many kinds of habitat from Clanwilliam to Humansdorp. (Aug-Oct)

There are about 30 species in the fynbos and Namaqualand regions of South Africa, of which 5 occur in this area. Two others bloom in the latter half of the year: *S. aquatica* of vleis and marshes with 2-7 white flowers per stem; and *S. flaccida* on rocky damp flats and slopes, with 1-3 yellow flowers on a solid stem.

IRIDACEAE

Anapalina triticea

An unbranched cormous geophyte producing a leafy stem to about 400 mm. The lowest leaves are very narrow at the base, broadening abruptly in the upper half, and brown at flowering time. The long-lasting flowers, 40-50 mm long and each with a 3-branched style, are borne in a dense spike. It occurs on rocky mountain slopes from Stellenbosch to Mossel Bay. (Jan-Apr)

There are 7 species endemic to the Cape mountains, of which 4 occur in this area. Another species with similar leaves, *A. burchellii*, with flowers 50-65 mm long may be found in the north of this area.

Anapalina nervosa

An unbranched cormous geophyte to 900 mm with a fan of leathery, flattened leaves up to 70 mm long. The flowers may be dull pink, pale or bright red or salmon, and are 45-60 mm long, with a much-elongated upper tepal. Common on stony or sandy mountain slopes and upland flats from Van Rhynsdorp to Port Elizabeth. (Dec-Mar)

The other species with leaves broad from the base, *A. pulchra*, lacks the elongated upper tepal.

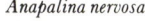

Amaryllis belladonna   *Spiloxene capensis*

Anapalina triticea   *Anapalina nervosa*

IRIDACEAE

Anomalesia cunonia   Rooipypie   Suikerkannetjie
A cormous geophyte 200-450 mm tall with several soft sword-shaped leaves. The long-lasting flowers are 50-60 mm long, including the extraordinarily long upper tepal, and the style is 3-branched. It occurs on the lower slopes of mountains near the sea and on coastal dunes from the Cape Peninsula to Knysna. (Sept-Oct)

There are 3 species confined to South Africa but this is the only species in this area.

The genus **Aristea** has crowded, narrow, flattened or cylindrical leaves. Flowers are carried in clusters up a branched or unbranched stem. Each flower lasts only one day but many appear successively over a period of weeks. Most have strikingly vivid blue flowers opening in bright sunlight. There are 50 species in sub-Saharan Africa and Madagascar, 30 of which occur in the Cape and 12 in this area.

Aristea major   Maagbossie
A stout and stiff-stemmed plant up to 1,5 m with flat leaves up to 20 mm wide. The crowded flowers are 12-16 mm long and emerge from brown or papery bracts which taper to a long thin point. It is common on steep lower mountain slopes from Piketberg to Caledon. (Oct-Dec)

Aristea spiralis
Flattened, usually unbranched flowering stems up to 500 mm long bear basal scimitar-shaped leaves up to 300 mm long. The exceptionally large greenish-white to pale blue, lilac, or deep blue flowers (up to 30 mm long) emerge from wide brown or green papery-edged bracts. It occurs in sandy places on mountain slopes from the Cape Peninsula to Willowmore. (Sept-Jan)

Aristea racemosa
A fairly slender plant with cylindrical rush-like leaves up to 500 mm long. The flowers are 12-18 mm long. They are borne in well-spaced few-flowered clusters along the stem. It occurs in sandy mountain soils from Paarl to George. (Oct-Jan)

Two other species in this area have cylindrical leaves: *A. oligocephala* with 25 mm long flowers in clusters at the tips of widely-forked branches, and *A. zeyheri* with mostly slender few-flowered heads.

Anomalesia cunonia

Aristea major

Aristea spiralis

Aristea racemosa

IRIDACEAE

The genus **Babiana** has hairy, pleated leaves and long-lasting, sessile flowers, which are blue or mauve in this area, with 3 style-branches. There are about 60 species, all but 2 in the Cape Province, of which 5 occur in this area.

Babiana ambigua
The 3-6 leaves are 40-80 mm in length and 3-10 mm wide. The fragrant flowers have a tube 10-19 mm long, with unequal lobes up to 40 mm long, and are borne on stems which curve close to the ground. The bracts are smooth or slightly hairy. Common on sandy flats and lower mountain slopes from Vanrhynsdorp to Riversdale. (July-Sept)

B. stricta var. *erectifolia* has leaves and flowering stems similarly arranged, but the flower lobes are equal and 15-25 mm long; while *B. montana* of the Klein River mountains blooms in winter and has large shaggy bracts.

Babiana purpurea
This erect-stemmed *Babiana* grows to 300 mm tall with a simple or branched stem. The leaves may be 60-120 mm long and 5-8 mm wide. The fragrant flowers occur in varying shades of mauve to purple-pink and the lobes are equal. Once common in clay ground at low altitudes, it is becoming rarer due to habitat destruction. Recorded from Caledon to Bredasdorp and Robertson. (Aug-Sept)

B. patersoniae has erect stems but unequal tepals.

The genus **Bobartia** has rushlike leaves and stems which resemble one another. The flowers are enclosed in narrow bract-wrapped bundles towards the end of the branches. Each flower lasts only one day, but several emerge successively from the same flowerhead. *Bobartia* becomes abundant in veld which is too frequently burnt or overgrazed. There are 14 species confined to sandy soils of the Cape and Natal, of which 4 occur in this area.

Bobartia longicyma   Grootbiesie
The cylindrical leaves and stems, equal in length and up to 1,8 m long, form large tufts when mature. The flowerheads are very slightly flattened and consist of 2-20 flower bundles up to 45 mm long and 7 mm wide. Recorded in the sandy lowlands from Palmiet River to Napier. (Aug-Nov)

Bobartia filiformis   Biesroei
Stems and leaves cylindrical, the stems being up to 500 mm long but the leaves a little shorter. The flowerheads have 1-3 bundles of flowers each. The flowers are unusual in that they open in dull weather and twilight, closing in bright sunlight, so this species is less noticed than the others. It is nevertheless common on sandy lower and midslopes of the mountains from the Cape Peninsula to Riversdale and Elim. (Sept-Dec)

Babiana ambigua

Babiana purpurea

Bobartia longicyma

Bobartia filiformis

IRIDACEAE

The genus **Geissorhiza** has soft bracts, green at least in the lower half, from which the stalkless long-lasting flowers emerge singly. The tepals are joined at the base to form a tube from which the long style, with 3-forked curling tip, extends. All 80 species occur in the Cape Province, of which about 20 are recorded in this area, several being very rare and local.

Geissorhiza ovata   Pink satin flower   Pienk satynblom
Variable in size, with sparsely branched or unbranched flowering stems up to 150 mm tall. The 2 lowest leaves are broad, oval and rounded at the tip. The flowers have a tube up to 27 mm long and the tepals are pink or white with a pink reverse. Recorded in sand on mountain slopes or coastal flats from Clanwilliam to Riversdale. (Aug-Oct)

Geissorhiza tenella
This plant, 100-300 mm tall, has sticky stems and 2 or 3 sticky leaves, round in cross-section and shorter than the stem. The irregular white or pink flowers borne 1-6 together in a spike, have a pink-veined reverse. They are 63-78 mm long and have a long straight tube and pointed lobes. It occurs on sandy flats and dunes from Darling to Bredasdorp. (Oct-Dec)

Geissorhiza aspera   Sysie   Syblom
The hairy stem of this species is a distinguishing feature. It may be 80-350 mm tall and bears 2-7 flowers which are about 10 mm long and blue to violet. Recorded near water or on sandy flats or slopes from the Gifberg to Bredasdorp. It is very common and can form carpets in suitable areas. (Aug-Sept)

The genus **Gladiolus** has long-lasting flowers arising between 2 green bracts. The style is 3-branched at the tip. One or more leaves arise from soil level, but other smaller leaves are also present as sheaths round the flowering stem. The genus is divided into those with 2 or more green leaves present at flowering time, those with only 1 green leaf, and those whose leaves appear at a different time from the flowers. There are about 150 species in Africa and Eurasia, of which about 105 occur in southern Africa and 21 in this area.

Gladiolus blommesteinii
The stem and single smooth basal leaf are 300-700 mm high, with 3 shorter stem leaves. The 1-4 flowers arise from clearly-veined bracts, and have distinctive lemon-throated red streaked lower lobes. It is common on the lower and middle mountain slopes from Worcester and the Hottentots Holland mountains to Bredasdorp, but has not been recorded in the Hermanus area. (Aug-Oct)

The similar *G. ornatus* has lemon markings outlined in red.

Geissorhiza ovata

Geissorhiza tenella

Geissorhiza aspera

Gladiolus blommesteinii

IRIDACEAE

Gladiolus carmineus   Hermanus cliff gladiolus
Usually about 300 mm tall, the unbranched flowering stem of this sweetly scented species bears 2-3 (occasionally up to 6) funnel-shaped flowers 65-100 mm long only 1 of which is usually open at a time. It produces its 1-3 flat trailing leaves after flowering is over. Recorded from Hangklip to Potberg on sandstone cliffs near the sea. (Feb-Apr)

Gladiolus bullatus   Caledon bluebell
This species may be 350-700 mm tall, with 1 short basal leaf and 2-3 stem leaves. The inflated bell-like flowers, 50 mm long, are borne 1-2 per stem. It is still fairly common despite being picked each year in masses for flower-shows, and is found on mountain slopes throughout this area and as far as Bredasdorp. (Aug-Oct)

Gladiolus debilis   Small painted lady
This species, 300-650 mm tall, has only 1 basal leaf, longer than the stem and 1,5-2 mm wide. The 1-4 flowers are 25-55 mm long and may be white or pink with red markings. It is fairly common on rocky mountain slopes among reeds or bushes from the Hottentots Holland to Bredasdorp, and is particularly abundant after veld fires. (Sept-Oct)

Gladiolus carneus   Large painted lady
A variable species which may grow to 1m in height, but is usually less. It produces a loose spike of 1-12 unscented flowers, 80 mm long with a 20 mm tube hidden by the bracts. It can be white, cream, pink or mauve and the 3 lower tepals, usually marked with red, are pointed. It may have up to 5 basal leaves at flowering time. It grows in rich sandy or marshy places from sea level to 1200 m, from Ceres to Riversdale. (Oct-Nov).

    The rather rare *G. undulatus* has a very similar colour and form, however, it has a tube 50-70 mm long, a flower up to 100 mm long, and the lower tepals are very long-tapered.

Gladiolus carmineus

Gladiolus bullatus

Gladiolus debilis

Gladiolus carneus

IRIDACEAE

Gladiolus punctulatus   Pypie
This non-fragrant, pale to deep pink, mauve or reddish 'pypie' grows 250-900 mm tall, with a single basal hairy leaf 2-6 mm broad and usually shorter than the stem. It occurs on the flats and lower mountain slopes from Piketberg to Riversdale and is common throughout this area. (June-Oct)

Gladiolus brevifolius   Pypie
This delicate plant is small-flowered and only occasionally scented. It becomes 150-650 mm tall, and is usually leafless when in flower, except for the sheathing leaves on the stem, the lowest of which is rust-tipped. It bears 3-10 flowers 30-50 mm long whose colour varies from pale to deep pink and (rarely) white or mauve, the lower lobes usually blotched with yellow or pink. It is very common on the lower sandy flats from Clanwilliam to Bredasdorp. (Mar-May)

    Other similar delicate autumn-blooming species are the blue or grey flowered fragrant *G. vaginatus* with orange throat, and the fragrant blue, grey or pink *G. pillansii* with a colourless sheathing leaf.

Gladiolus gracilis   Pypie
This variable, usually fragrant pypie is between 200-750 mm tall with 1 characteristically harsh-textured basal leaf. The 1-8 flowers are 24-40 mm long and the colour varies from pale blue to grey-mauve to pink with cream markings. It occurs on sandy flats or lower mountain slopes among reeds and bushes from Malmesbury to Heidelberg and throughout this area. (May-Sept)

Gladiolus maculatus   Brown Afrikander   Bruin Afrikander
This 300-800 mm tall plants bears 1-3 (occasionally 4) very fragrant funnel-shaped flowers 50-100 mm long. It has no leaves at flowering time. The dull colour can vary from yellow to pinkish to brown-spotted and streaked with dark brown, purple or red. It grows on lower mountain slopes of the coastal belt from Ceres to the eastern Cape. (Mar-July)

    Another large, brown, spring-blooming 'Afrikander', *G. liliaceus*, bears 1 basal and 3 sheath leaves. It has the unusual characteristic of appearing deep mauve or blue at dusk and developing a strong fragrance. Another very fragrant species, the greenish-yellow *G. acuminatus* blooms in spring and has 5-10 leaves.

Gladiolus punctulatus

Gladiolus brevifolius

Gladiolus gracilis

Gladiolus maculatus

IRIDACEAE

Hesperantha falcata   Aandblom
A cormous geophyte 60-300 mm tall with 3-5 narrow curved or straight leaves which are only half as long as the flowering stems. The 1-8 long-tubed flowers arise singly from soft green or perhaps red-flushed bracts. The style forks into 3 long branches at the mouth of the flower. The flowers are white or yellow, flushed red, pink or brown below, the white forms opening and becoming sweetly-scented at dusk; the yellow forms are without scent and open during the day. Widespread from Nieuwoudtville to the Cape Peninsula and east to Port Elizabeth. (July-Oct)

About 55 species occur south of the Sahara, of which 36 are found in the Cape and 5 in this area.

Homeria bulbillifera   Aasuintjie   Uintjiestulp
A cormous, usually much-branched, erect or trailing plant to about 600 mm tall. It has 1 long basal leaf 5-10 mm wide, arising close to the ground. The unscented flowers are coloured pale to deep yellow, pale pink or orange-flushed, and are 30-48 mm long with a narrow green-spotted dark yellow cup. It is distinctive in that as flowering ends clusters of cormlets develop in the axils of the stem leaves. It occurs in coastal sand or limestone from the Cape Peninsula to the eastern Cape. (Sept-Nov)

There are about 31 species confined to southern Africa, of which 5 occur in this area.

Ixia dubia   Kalossies
The stem is 200-750 mm tall, usually unbranched, with 5-7 leaves 100-500 mm long and 1,5-8 mm wide. The short-tubed flowers are deep gold to orange, often with a dark eye, and usually reddish on the reverse. Fairly common on sandy flats and slopes from Piketberg to Caledon. (Oct-Dec)

There are 45 species occurring in the Cape Province of which 9 occur in this area. A second yellow-flowered Ixia occurs here, *I. odorata* with sulphur-yellow to lemon-yellow sweetly scented flowers in the spring.

Ixia micrandra   Pink Ixia   Kalossie
This species has a stem 200-600 mm tall with 2-3 more or less cylindrical leaves 120-300 mm long. The flowers, 13-25 mm long, are white to pink. It occurs on mountain slopes and hills in the Caledon and Bredasdorp areas. (July-Sept)

All the other white, pink, mauve or blue-coloured ixias in this area have broad leaves except *I. flexuosa*, whose faintly-scented flowers in the same colour group are carried on a flower stem angled between the flowers, and *I. cochlearis* of Jonkershoek with rose or salmon flowers. Of the broad-leaved species *I. trinervata* of the Elgin area has bright to deep pink flowers.

Hesperantha falcata

Homeria bulbillifera

Ixia dubia

Ixia micrandra

IRIDACEAE

The genus **Moraea** is characterised by cormous plants with long, usually narrow leaves which may be attached anywhere along the flowering stem from ground level to just below the flowers. The flowers are usually short-lived, symmetrical and iris-like and have 6 (sometimes only 3) tepals. The centre of the flower is occupied by 3 stamens secluded beneath 3 forked, more or less frilly or crested, petal-like structures which are the style-branches. There are 110 species in sub-Saharan Africa, of which 55 occur in the Cape Province and 20 in this area.

Moraea angusta
This large-flowered species grows up to 400 mm high with an unbranched stem which is often sticky at the joints. A single cylindrical hairless leaf is attached near the ground. The non-scented, pale yellow (occasionally grey-blue) flower 30-50 mm long, is veined purplish below and has a clear yellow nectar guide. The pollen is usually orange-red, sometimes yellow. Occurring most often after fires on lower mountain slopes, in sandy or rocky soil, from the Cedarberg to Knysna. (Aug-Nov)

Similar cream or yellow-flowered species are the unscented *M. anomala* which, however, is never sticky and favours clay ground; and the sticky *M. bituminosa* with 2 thin flat leaves.

Moraea lugubris   Kersblakertjie
A plant up to 160 mm tall, with 2 or more non-hairy, dissimilar leaves; the lower is narrow and attached at ground level, the upper, much shorter and broad-based, is attached just beneath the flowers. The bright blue flowers are up to 18 mm long with red pollen and feathery styles unique in the genus. Local from Nieuwoudtville to Bredasdorp, and throughout this area, it occurs from sea level to mid-altitudes, most often on damp sandy soils, but also on decomposed granite. (Aug-Nov)

Moraea tripetala
A usually unbranched slender plant to 500 mm tall. It has 1 narrow leaf longer than the stem. The flowers are pale mauve to deep violet, and have 3 large outer tepals, bearded within. The other 3 tepals are minute. Widespread and common on flats and slopes from Nieuwoudtville to George. (Aug-Dec)

Moraea tricuspidata
Usually 250-600 mm tall and branched with 1 narrow, flattened, hairless leaf attached at ground level. The white or cream flowers, emerging from soft green bracts with threadlike tips, are speckled and slightly hairy within; they have 3 horizontal outer tepals, up to 30 mm long. The 3 inner tepals are very small with a whiplash coiled tip. Occurring most often on lower mountain slopes on heavy clay soils from the Cape Peninsula to Grahamstown, it blooms after veld fires. (Sept-Nov)

A similar species, the sweet-scented *M. viscaria* resembles the white form, but has a purple-flushed flower and is sticky.

Moraea angusta

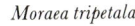

Moraea lugubris

Moraea tripetala

Moraea tricuspidata

IRIDACEAE

Moraea neglecta
A plant with an unbranched stem 200-500 mm tall, sometimes sticky. The single leaf is longer than the stem. The intensely bright yellow flower with 2 black-dotted nectar-guides has a sweet vanilla scent. It occurs mainly on sandy flats near the coast from the Olifants River mouth to Stanford, and also in the Cedarberg and Nieuwoudtville area. (Sept-Nov)

Other yellow-flowered moraeas with which it can be confused are the non-sticky hairy yellow forms of *M. papilionacea*, with nectar-guides outlined in green or red, and the 1 m tall non-sticky hairless *M. bellendenii*, with bright yellow flowers and one basal trailing leaf, preferring sandy soils.

Moraea fugax
Usually up to 500 mm tall, the illustration shows a dwarf form in wind-blown sand. It has 1 narrow trailing leaf (occasionally 2), longer than the stem, and attached just below the flowers. The flowers may be white, yellow or blue, about 24-40 mm long, with yellow honey-guides and a strong sweet scent. It is found mainly in sandy coastal areas from Namaqualand to Mossel Bay. (Aug-Dec)

Other mauve or blue-flowered species in the area include *M. villosa* (peacock moraea) with 3 large tepals having a band of contrasting colour and conspicuous honey-guides. There are 2 stemless species; the unscented *M. tricolor*, mauve, yellow or red, has 3 leaves, and the sweet-scented *M. ciliata* may be blue, white, yellow or pale green, with 2-6 leaves in a fan.

Nivenia stokoei
A shrub with fibrous roots and woody stem to 600 mm. The leaves form fan-shaped clusters, each leaf being up to 90 mm long and 1,5-3 mm broad. The terminal gentian-blue flowers are up to 60 mm long with a tube 25-40 mm long. A common but very local plant of the lower stony slopes above Betty's Bay and Kleinmond. (Feb-Mar)

Nivenia levynsiae
A delicate rounded shrublet to 250 mm tall, from a thick underground base. It has fans of blue-green leaves each up to 40 mm long and 1-2 mm wide. Each flower is 18-20 mm long, with a tube up to 15 mm long. The heads of blue flowers are raised above the adjacent leaves. Found only on the summits of the mountains from Kogelberg to Kleinmond, it inhabits dry rocky ridges. (Dec-Feb)

A third species, *N. concinna*, occurring in the northeast inland part of this area has bright blue flowers with a tube 20 mm long, the flowers nestling among the leaves.

Moraea neglecta

Moraea fugax

Nivenia stokoei

Nivenia levynsiae

IRIDACEAE

Tritonia cooperi
A cormous geophyte with 4-6 leaves arising from ground level and 1 or 2 smaller stem leaves; they may be flattened or, in drier areas, round in cross-section. The irregular, sessile flowers are borne in clusters on unbranched or branched stems 400-600 mm tall and emerge from a pair of brown, blunt-tipped bracts. The 45-80 mm long flowers are white, cream or pale pink, darkening with age. The 3 stamens arch in one direction under the upper lobes. It occurs on sandy mountain slopes from Worcester to Caledon and Riversdale. (Nov-Dec)

There are 30 species in southern Africa and 3 in this area: the smallest *T. flabellifolia* has long tapering bracts and stamens which do not arch in one direction; *T. crispa* has leaves with ruffled edges.

Lapeirousia corymbosa   Koringblommetjie
A cormous geophyte 50-300 mm high with a single basal leaf much longer than the stem and a few smaller leaves on the stem. The long-tubed flowers, blue with a white star, but sometimes cream or white, are 20 mm long and have a 6-branched style. They grow in sand or clay from the Cape Peninsula to Tulbagh and Elim. (Sept-Nov)

There are about 35 species in Africa of which about 25 occur in southern Africa and 3 in this area.

Romulea hirsuta
A low-growing geophyte with a corm and threadlike, often finely-hairy leaves to 300 mm in length. The apricot to dark rose flowers are 20-45 mm long with a yellow cup. The tepal lobes have a dark middle vein. The flowers emerge from 2 green bracts, the inner having a brown or white translucent edge. This is a widely distributed common species from Ceres and Saldanha Bay to Bredasdorp, in sandy soil from the coast to 900 m. (Aug-Oct)

There are about 95 species from the Mediterranean region southwards through Africa, of which 70 occur in South Africa and 10 in this area. The closely related *R. triflora*, widespread in sandy loams at low altitude, differs mainly in having hairless leaves and bright golden yellow flowers.

Romulea rosea   Froetang Knikkertjies
A stemless geophyte with several threadlike, rather stiff hairless leaves up to 360 mm long. The flower stalks are 30-80 mm long and the pale lilac-pink or sometimes white flowers with a yellowish cup, are up to 25 mm long. The tepal lobes are yellowish-green and dark-striped on the reverse. Common on sandy flats especially in disturbed places from Nieuwoudtville to Port Elizabeth. (July-Nov)

It is a proclaimed weed in Australia, and is naturalised in Tristan da Cunha, St Helena and Guernsey.

Tritonia cooperi

Lapeirousia corymbosa

Romulea hirsuta

Romulea rosea

IRIDACEAE

Pillansia templemanii
A cormous evergreen geophyte to 1,2 m with 1 erect hairless, ribbed leaf 10 mm broad. The open cluster of 10 mm long short-tubed flowers with 6-branched styles is borne on a branched stem. Occurring on the lower stony slopes and flats from False Bay to Hermanus where it forms large colonies. It seldom flowers except after fire, when it may be seen in spectacular sheets of colour. (Oct-Nov)

There is only 1 species.

Sparaxis grandiflora   Fluweelblom   Botterblom
An unbranched geophyte 80-450 mm tall bearing a few cormlets in the lowest joints of the stems after flowering. There are 6-10 outcurving leaves 4-13 mm wide and shorter than the stem. The 1-6 long-lasting flowers are 35-45 mm long and may be cream, red-purple, violet or yellow with a yellow, purple or black eye, with or without dark markings. Occurring on damp clay flats from Clanwilliam to Caledon. (Aug-Sept)

There are 6 species confined to the fynbos, of which only 1 other occurs in this area.

The genus **Watsonia** includes species which are among the tallest and stoutest members of the family. They have sword-like leaves and sessile flowers with a 6-branched stigma. The tepals form a narrow tube widening above to 6 more or less equal lobes. Flowering in most species is profuse after veld fires. There are about 50 species confined to South Africa, of which 11 occur in this area.

Watsonia stenosiphon
A dainty 300-500 mm tall plant whose rather soft leaves have inconspicuous veins. The unbranched flowering stems bear stem-leaves which may have cormlets in their axils. They bear a number of bright orange, apricot, pink or mauve flowers arising upright out of stem-clasping bracts. The flowers have a 35 mm long straight tube and wide-spreading 20 mm long lobes. It occurs on sandy coastal flats from Kleinmond to Potberg. (Sept-Nov).

Watsonia schlechteri
Sturdy plants, 300-900 mm tall with leaves 320-360 mm long and 6-9 mm broad, whose edges are as strikingly thickened as the midrib. The unbranched flowering stems bear numerous 60-70 mm long flowers arising out of 25 mm long bracts which do not clasp the stem. The cylindrical, outcurving flowers have narrow lobes half as long as the tube. They occur as solitary plants scattered on rocky, well-drained mountain slopes from Bain's Kloof to Swellendam and the Klein Swartberg. (Nov-Feb)

Pillansia templemanii

Sparaxis grandiflora

Watsonia stenosiphon

Watsonia schlechteri

IRIDACEAE

Watsonia borbonica   Suurkanol
A common clump-forming plant to 2 m with firm glossy leaves 500-700 mm long and 20-40 mm wide. The faintly scented pink or purple 50-70 mm long flowers, borne on sturdy, much-branched stems, emerge from bracts which are often sticky within but do not clasp the stem. The flower tube widens conspicuously to the throat and bears wide lobes equal in length to the tube or longer. Common on mountain slopes from Worcester and the Cape Peninsula to Bredasdorp, it blooms in late spring and is especially profuse after fires. (Oct-Dec)

Thereianthus bracteolatus
A cormous geophyte to 300 mm high with cylindrical leaves up to 150 mm long, sometimes withering at flowering time. A sturdy, unbranched flowering stem with hard brown bracts carries 7-14 flowers each about 7 mm long, in a spirally arranged spike. It occurs on well-drained soils at a wide range of altitudes, from Clanwilliam to Bredasdorp. (Sept-Nov)

There are 7 species confined to the southwestern Cape, of which 3 occur in this area. *T. juncifolius* has rush-like leaves often overtopping the flowering stems and occurs in wet sites; and *T. spicatus* has a single flat leaf from ground level and 3 progressively shorter stem leaves.

Ferraria crispa   Spinnekopblom Uiltjie
This 200-800 mm tall cormous geophyte has slightly fleshy, overlapping leaves partly concealing the branched, straight or slightly twisted stem. Each flower, about 35 mm across, lasts for only one day and is carrion-scented. Recorded from sandy and loamy places from Clanwilliam to Willowmore and along the coast from Kleinmond to Mossel Bay. (July-Oct)

Tritoniopsis lata
A cormous geophyte with 1-3 long narrow leaves emerging from a neck of wiry fibres at ground level, and 3-5 smaller stem leaves. The irregular 29-44 mm long flowers are borne in a short spike at the tip of an unbranched stem, arising singly from dry brownish bracts. It occurs in sandy and rocky places on the mountains from Tulbagh to Caledon. (Feb-May)

There are 14 species in the southwestern Cape, of which 7 occur in this area. Other pink-flowered species include *T. pulchella* and *T. ramosa* with large flowers on branched stems, the upper tepals of the former being clearly broader than the lower; and the dull pink *T. dodii..*

Watsonia borbonica

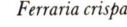

Thereianthus bracteolatus

Ferraria crispa

Tritoniopsis lata

ORCHIDACEAE

An extremely varied family with a unique and complex flower structure. All species in this area are terrestrial and produce new leaves each year, usually from a tuber or rhizome. Each flower has 3 sepals and 3 petals borne above a 3-chambered ovary, the sepals often resembling petals. In most species, the flower twists so that the third sepal, instead of being at the bottom of the flower, forms a hood at the top. The third petal then takes its place at the bottom, being known as the lip and is often variously fringed, crested or lobed and may bear 1 or 2 spurs.

Disa uniflora   Red disa   Rooi disa
This best known and possibly most beautiful of all the disas cannot be mistaken when its glowing red, (occasionally pink or yellow) colour is seen in the spray of a waterfall or beside a mountain stream. The plants grow up to 600 mm tall with a number of stem leaves. The tiny petals are enclosed within the hooded, spurred upper sepal. The short narrow lip at the front of the flower can just be seen in the illustration. It is still fairly widespread in the southwestern Cape owing possibly to its often inaccessible habitat. (Jan-Mar)

There are about 80 species of *Disa* in Africa and Madagascar of which 70 occur in South Africa and 27 in this area.

Herschelianthe graminifolia   Blue disa
Slender-stemmed to 1 m with 4-6 basal grasslike leaves, and some short stem leaves. The single-spurred, sweetly-scented flowers are blue with 2 green petals visible inside the hooded upper sepal. Found on dry sunny mountain slopes in dense vegetation between 300-1000 m in the southwestern Cape. (Jan-Mar)

There are 16 species in Africa of which 6 may occur in this area. The very similar *H. purpurascens* is found usually below 300 m and blooms earlier in spring.

Disa pillansii
A slender tuberous geophyte to 300 mm with several broad leaves arising from ground level, and some loosely enfolding the stem. The globose flowers, about 20-28 mm across, have a nipple-like spur. Occurring rather infrequently at streamsides and in mossy seepages in the summer cloud zone of the Caledon district between 500-1500 m. (Dec)

Disa vaginata
A slender tuberous geophyte to 200 mm with leaves only on the stem, and 3-10 rose-spotted single-spurred flowers about 10-12 mm across. Occurring as isolated plants or small groups in dry stony soil or in moss, on rocks between 300-1300 m, it is widespread in the mountains of the southern and western Cape. (Nov-Dec)

Disa uniflora

Herschelianthe graminifolia

Disa pillansii

Disa vaginata

ORCHIDACEAE

Schizodium obliquum   Kapotjie
A delicate wiry-stemmed geophyte to 300 mm, with typically, a few "hairpin" bends at the base of the stem. It has a few basal leaves, the others closely sheathing the stem. It may have 2-9 pale pink flowers with lobes 5-10 mm long and 1 flattened spur about two-thirds as long. Occurring on seasonally wet deep sand between sea level and 300 m in the extreme southwest Cape. (Aug-Sept)

The genus is endemic to the western and southern Cape, having 6 species, 4 of which probably occur in this area.

Pterygodium catholicum   Moederkappie
A slender tuberous geophyte 300 mm tall with oblong leaves up to 110 mm long. It has a few-flowered head of greenish-yellow flowers, sometimes red-flushed, with a strong pungent scent. Flowers lack spurs. It occurs in open fynbos from 50-1600 m in the southwest Cape. (Sept-Dec)

There are about 15 species found in South Africa, 7 of them in this area. All have yellowish to greenish-yellow flowers.

Eulophia litoralis
An erect, rather slender plant to 650 mm. The leaves are borne on a separate shoot next to the flowering stem but are not always present at flowering time. There may be 6-27 flowers in a loose raceme, each with a puff of yellow hairs in the throat. It is found on coastal sands and lower mountain slopes in the south and southwest Cape. (Nov-Jan)

There are about 200 species throughout the tropics and sub-tropics, of which only 3 occur in this area.

Bonatea speciosa   Moederkappie   Oktoberlelie
A sturdy tuberous geophyte to 1 m with a leafy stem. The dark green sharply pointed leaves measure up to 130 mm by 40 mm. The green and white flowers with a deeply lobed lip and narrow petals are carried in a fairly dense head. It is quite frequently seen in sandy soil in coastal scrub and forest margins from sea level to 1200 m, from Malmesbury along the coastal belt to the eastern Cape. (June-Feb)

Although there are about 20 species in Arabia and Africa, there are no others in this area.

Schizodium obliquum

Pterygodium catholicum

Eulophia litoralis

Bonatea speciosa

ORCHIDACEAE

Satyrium. This is the only genus illustrated here in which the flowers are not twisted, and hence the 'lip' is at the top of the hooded, 2 spurred flower. The sepals and petals are often joined to the lip. Over 80 species are found in southern and tropical Africa, India, Tibet and China, of which about 15 occur in this area, some of them rare.

Satyrium carneum   Rooitrewwa
A vigorous sturdy plant to 800 mm with 2 very broad leaves, up to 230 mm long, pressed flat to the ground, and several more enfolding the stem. The crowded unscented flowers, pale-pink to rose in colour are 35 mm across with 2 18-25 mm long spurs. Local and increasingly rare in coastal dunes and in fynbos near the sea, from 15-300 m in the southwestern Cape; it may still be seen in dense stands after veld fires, for example at Betty's Bay. (Sept-Nov)

Satyrium coriifolium   Ewwa-trewwa
A robust plant to 770 mm with 2 to 4 thick, stiff leaves enfolding the stem. The bright orange unscented flowers form a dense elongated spike. The specimen illustrated opposite is still mostly in bud. Each flower is about 26 mm across with 2 spurs 9 mm long. Occurring abundantly on coastal sands and clayey mountain foothills, from sea level to 750 m, though now becoming rare due to development and encroachment by alien weeds. It is recorded from the southwestern Cape to the eastern Cape. (Aug-Dec)

Satyrium odorum   Ruiktrewwa
A robust tuberous geophyte to 560 mm with 2 to 6 spreading, fleshy leaves sheathing the stem. The pungently-scented (some say carnation-scented!) greenish flowers form a loose spike of up to 45 flowers each about 18 mm across. The 2 spurs, 13-18 mm long, stand well away from the flower. It occurs on sandy soils in protected places at low altitudes in the southwestern and southern Cape. (Aug-Nov)

Satyrium lupulinum
A slender-stemmed plant to 500 mm with up to 3 leaves, 20-80 mm long, near the ground and a number of others clasping the stem. The rather crowded flowers have a soapy pungent scent and are about 13-20 mm across with 2 spurs 15-18 mm long. The colour varies from dull yellowish-green tinged with purple to entirely dull purplish-brown, as in the specimen illustrated (typical of those in the Hermanus area). Occurring on the coastal flats and mountains from the southwest to eastern Cape; it blooms most freely after fires. (Aug-Dec)

Satyrium carneum

Satyrium coriifolium

Satyrium odorum

Satyrium lupulinum

ORICHIDACEAE

Disa tripetaloides
A slender plant to 600 mm with lance-shaped leaves arising at ground level gradually grading into the stem leaves. It has many single-spurred flowers about 14-33 mm across, distributed along most of the length of the stem. It is most often found along streams or in moss on damp mountain slopes, from sea level to 1000 m from the southwestern to the eastern Cape and Natal. (Nov-Jan)

Monadenia comosa
A plant with a slightly twisted stem 80-600 mm high bearing 2, occasionally 3, semi-erect basal leaves and a number of smaller leaves close to the stem. It carries an open cluster of lime-green flowers, each with a single spur up to 24 mm long. Found on half-shaded rock ledges or in damp crevices on the mountains up to 2000 m from Cedarberg to Uniondale. (Sept-Nov)

There are 21 species in South Africa of which 11 occur in this area.

Pterygodium alatum
A slender plant to 180 mm tall, with elliptical leaves and a number of pungently-scented flowers about 11 mm across. The lip has 2 broad lobes and a narrow spur 6-7 mm long. It occurs in low fynbos from 30-900 m throughout the southwestern Cape. (Aug-Sept)

Disperis capensis   Moederkappie
A slender plant to 430 mm with 2 narrow leaves up to 90 mm long. It usually has a single flower in which the petals are joined to the uppermost sepal, forming a hood with a long erect spur. The lateral sepals are long and narrow with recurved tips. It is usually purplish in colour but this illustration shows a less usual greenish-white form. Occurring in open well-drained fynbos from near sea level to 900 m in the western and southern Cape. (June-Sept)

There are about 75 species from Africa to New Guinea, of which about 30 occur in South Africa and 7 in this area.

Disa tripetaloides

Monadenia comosa

Pterygodium alatum

Disperis capensis

PROTEACEAE

Aulax umbellata
This is a genus in which male and female flowers occur on different plants. The male is illustrated here, showing the short bright yellow spikes of its flowers. The female is less showy, having rounded heads in clusters at the tips of the branches, partly hidden by the leaves. The flowers are borne on sturdy shrubs up to 2 m tall and have leaves up to 15 mm broad at the top, tapering towards the base. Frequent, sometimes in dense stands on lower sandy slopes from Cape Peninsula to Riversdale. (Dec-June)

There are 2 other species, both occurring in this area: the many-stemmed *A. pallasia* which sprouts from a fire-resistant stump after veld fires, and the single-stemmed *A. cancellata* with needle-like leaves.

Diastella divaricata
A low, sprawling, mat-forming single-stemmed shrublet covering an area 1-3 m in diameter. The small, oval leaves are clothed when young with long, black hairs. The pink flowerheads, up to 15 mm across, are surrounded by silky bracts. Occurring from 300-1200 m in small scattered groups on mountain slopes from Franschhoek to Hermanus. (Jan-Dec)

There are 7 species, all in the southwest Cape, of which 3 occur in this area.

Diastella fraterna
This plant is very similar to the previous species but is more upright in habit and has white flowerheads, surrounded by pale bracts which become papery with age. It is confined to the mountains behind Kleinmond and the lower Palmiet River catchment from sea level to 450 m and blooms throughout the year.

The sweet-scented *D. thymelaeoides*, an erect shrub over 1 m tall, is found at Pringle Bay and Hangklip.

Spatalla curvifolia
A rounded, woody, single-stemmed shrublet to 750 mm with needlelike, usually curved leaves, 25-50 mm long. The densely-hairy creamy-white flowers are arranged singly in a rather open terminal cluster. It grows socially on well-drained sandy or rocky slopes from sea level to 330 m from Steenbras to Bredasdorp. (Jan-Dec)

There are 20 species confined to the fynbos, of which 7 others have been recorded from this area. The dense pinkish heads of *S. mollis*, with its crowded needle-like leaves, are conspicuous in high altitude swamps; *S. racemosa*, locally common from Houhoek to Hermanus, is a smaller, more laxly branched shrub.

Aulax umbellata

Diastella divaricata

Diastella fraterna

Spatalla curvifolia

PROTEACEAE

The genus **Leucadendron**, the "sunshine proteas" or "tolbosse", consists of about 80 species of large shrubs with male and female flowers on separate plants. It occurs mainly in the fynbos area of the Cape but extends into Natal. Fourteen species occur in this area. They may be single-stemmed shrubs which regenerate from seed, or many-stemmed, resprouting from large persistent stumps after a veld fire has destroyed the above ground parts. The female flowers are gathered into cone-like heads at the ends of branches. Some species release their fruits as soon as they are ripe; others retain them in the cone for several years. The male plants are often rather unlike the females. Their leaves are often somewhat smaller, and the tiny flowers are carried in dense terminal heads.

Leucadendron rubrum (male)   Tolletjiesbos

Erect single-stemmed shrubs to 2,5 m with slender branches. The leaves are up to 34 mm long and 4,5 mm broad. Bright yellow inflorescences are borne in abundance at the ends of the branches. (May-Sept)

Leucadendron rubrum (female)

Similar in height to the male, but with stouter branches and larger leaves. The fruits are held in a top-shaped cone which remains on the plant for a number of years. The fresh cones are unusual in having the stigmas visible in a small tuft at the top of the cone. Widespread, sometimes occurring in dense stands, from the Gifberg in the north to Uniondale in the east, it favours the drier sandy slopes of the interior mountains. (May-Sept)

Leucadendron tinctum (female)

Spreading, single-stemmed shrubs to 1,3 m. The oblong, bluegreen leaves are up to 115 mm long by 45 mm broad in the female and slightly less in the male. They become larger and more crowded towards the tips of the branches forming a loose red and yellow-flushed cup around the flower heads. In the female plant the flowers are borne in a yellowish cone, later becoming reddish, with a strong spicy smell. The cones ripen and release their fruits within a few months. The fruits are buried by ants. Occurring in fairly dense stands on stony, acid sands in the Caledon and Bredasdorp districts, it has been recorded throughout this area. (July-Aug)

Leucadendron spissifolium   Vleigeelbos

A variable, many-stemmed shrub to 1,3 m with glossy leaves up to 80 mm long by 17 mm broad, broadest towards the often hair-tufted tips; rather smaller in the male and becoming ivory or pale green and broader around the flower heads. The female cones redden as they mature, and are held until the stems of the parent plant are killed by fire, when they open and release the winged seeds. Occurring in sandy soils in damp places and on south-facing slopes as scattered plants, from sea level to 1400 m from Clanwilliam and Worcester to Riversdale. (Aug-Oct)

Leucadendron rubrum (male)   *Leucadendron rubrum (female)*

Leucadendron tinctum (female)   *Leucadendron spissifolium*

PROTEACEAE

Leucadendron gandogeri — Berggeelbos
A robust rounded single-stemmed shrub to 1,6 m with the leaves of the female plant 20-26 mm broad and 60-100 mm long, and those of the male slightly smaller. Towards the tips of the branches they turn bright yellow and form a loose colourful cup around the flowerheads. The smooth hairless female cones are surrounded at the base by small recurved brown bracts. They remain for many years or until the death of the parent plant, when they release the winged fruits. Note that the male and female flowers shown in the illustration were not growing on the same plant. Often found in dense stands on stony, sandy lower slopes, it occurs from Stellenbosch to Bredasdorp. (Aug-Sept)

Mimetes hirtus
An erect shrub to 1,5 m with soft, hairy, loosely overlapping leaves. The straight flowers are grouped near the tips of the branches and project in clusters of 9-14 from the angle of a green leaf. The entire head is topped by rusty-pink leaves. Recorded in marshes and wet seepages usually on the coastal plain near the sea, from the Cape Peninsula to Swellendam. (May-Nov)

With recent coastal housing development it is a likely candidate for extinction.

Mimetes cucullatus
A dense shrub up to about 1,5 m tall, with numerous branches emerging at the base, from which it rapidly regenerates after veld fires. The crowded overlapping leaves are 25-55 mm long and 5-20 mm broad. The upper leaves, from which the flowerheads emerge, become bright red. Common and widespread throughout our area and ranging from the Cedarberg in the north to Baviaanskloof in the east, it may bloom at any time of the year.

The genus **Leucospermum** consists of 46 species of shrubby plants known as 'pincushion proteas' or 'luisies', occurring mainly in the fynbos regions of the Cape Province, but one extending into Zimbabwe. Thirteen have been recorded from this area. The seeds have oily protuberances which are carried down into their burrows by ants, and eaten. The seeds escape undamaged and remain viable below ground for many years and germinate when conditions are favourable.

Leucospermum oleifolium
An erect, single-stemmed rounded shrub growing to 1 m, with lance-shaped leaves up to 60 mm by 25 mm. The flowerheads, each 25-40 mm across, are grouped in clusters of from 2 to 5. The flowers open bright yellow and turn crimson with age, each cluster usually containing a range of different shades, and remaining colourful for up to two months. Occurring in a variety of habitats from sea level to 1000 m, often in dense stands, it has been recorded from Bain's Kloof to Hangklip and on to the Riviersonderend mountains but not at Hermanus. (Aug-Jan)

Leucadendron gandogeri

Mimetes hirtus

Mimetes cucullatus

Leucospermum oleifolium

PROTEACEAE

Leucospermum gracile
A mat-forming shrub to 1,5 m across with a single main stem and leaves 20-45 mm by 2-5 mm. The top-shaped, yellow flowerheads, 25-30 mm across, become greenish with age. It is still abundant on the mountains at Onrus and Hermanus but has been exterminated from the Bot River area, formerly its most northerly habitat. It prefers south-facing aspects from 100-330 m but may occur up to 1200 m in well-drained sands. (July-Dec)

Leucospermum prostratum
A trailing perennial with numerous slender unbranched stems up to 2 m long. The olive-green leaves are up to 40 mm long by 2-6 mm broad. Clusters of up to 3 spherical, sweetly-scented flowerheads, 20-25 mm in diameter, open bright yellow and become orange with age. It occurs mainly on sandy coastal flats and has been recorded from Kogelberg eastwards to Bredasdorp. (July-Dec)

Another mat-forming *Leucospermum* is the sweetly-scented *L. hypophyllocarpodendron* with bright yellow inflorescences and narrow erect leaves, which may be found in the Stellenbosch area.

Leucospermum gueinzii
A coarse hairy shrub to 3 m with a single main stem and smooth bright green leaves up to 100 mm by 30 mm. The deep orange flowerheads, up to 140 mm across, occur in groups of 1-3 and become bright crimson with age. It occurs in moist sheltered kloofs near streams on heavy clay soils from 300-1000 m on the Hottentots Holland mountains from Jonkershoek to Sir Lowry's Pass. It is probably extinct at Houhoek, the furthest east of its range. (Aug-Dec)

Leucospermum lineare
Two forms of this plant occur, the more usual being one with a sprawling habit and golden yellow flowers. A local, more erect form, with deep orange flowers is found at Franschhoek. The plants have narrow leaves 40-100 mm long and only 2-7 mm wide, with flowerheads up to 90 mm across. They are usually solitary but sometimes in groups of 2-3. It occurs on granite-derived clay and gravelly soils between 300-1000 m in the mountains from Bain's Kloof to Jonkershoek, but is nowhere common. (July-Jan)

Leucospermum gracile

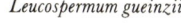

Leucospermum prostratum

Leucospermum gueinzii

Leucospermum lineare

PROTEACEAE

Leucospermum truncatulum Patrysbos
A slender single-stemmed shrub to 2 m with stiff, sparse branches concealed by the grey hairy leaves. These lack the gland-tipped points of most other *Leucospermums*. The small pincushion flowerheads, about 20 mm across, are yellow at first but turn crimson with age. It is common on the lower coastal slopes from the Hottentots Holland to Bredasdorp, usually in large open colonies. (Aug-Dec)

Protea is a genus of 114 species occurring in Africa of which 28 occur in this area. Varying in habit from trees to apparently stemless shrublets, their bisexual flowers are grouped in bowl-shaped heads surrounded by colourful bracts.

Protea cynaroides Giant protea   King protea   Bergroos
Groot suikerroos
Our national flower and the protea depicted on our coinage, this 2 m coarse, sparsely-branched shrub has a fire-resistant stump. The leathery leaves are up to 300 mm long, with long well-developed leafstalks. The enormous flowerheads measure up to 300 mm across and vary in colour from pale greenish cream to a soft deep pink. It occurs on sandstone from sea level to 1500 m from the Cedarberg to the Cape Peninsula and on to the eastern Cape, wherever the annual rainfall exceeds 400 mm. It may be found in bloom at any time of year.

Protea acaulos Aardroos
A prostrate shrublet with a few trailing stems, resprouting after fire. The smooth, oval leaves, all directed to one side of the stem, are variable in size; 60-250 mm long by 10-70 mm wide and taper gradually to the base. The cupshaped, 60 mm wide flowerheads have hairless, slightly incurving topmost bracts, which later curve backwards to reveal the brownish tips of the flower cluster within. Widespread from the Cedarberg to Bredasdorp and throughout this area, it favours sandy or granite-derived soils from sea level to 1500 m. (June-Nov)

Protea longifolia
Single-stemmed shrubs about 1,5 m high, with crowded, narrow leaves, 90-200 mm long. The flowerheads, 80-160 mm long, have smooth translucent green, white or pink bracts and a long-pointed black beard of flowers within. It occurs in open stands between Sir Lowry's Pass and Cape Agulhas on low hills and mountain slopes to 150 m, rarely higher, on sand or clayey ironstone gravel. (May-Sept)

Leucospermum truncatulum

Protea cynaroides

Protea acaulos

Protea longifolia

PROTEACEAE

Protea burchellii
A 1-2 m tall branching shrub with long narrow leaves 70-170 mm by 7-20 mm. The flowerheads are up to 110 mm long and surrounded by cream or pink bracts fringed with brown, black, or occasionally white hairs. The bracts are so shiny they appear greasy, and curve inwards over the much shorter, dark-bearded flowers within. It occurs on lower slopes and valleys of the southwestern Cape on a variety of soils. Extinct in the Cape Peninsula, it may still be seen in the western part of this area from Franschhoek to Sir Lowry's Pass. (June-Aug)

Protea neriifolia
An erect tree-like shrub to 3 m, branching close to the ground from a single strong trunk. It has bright green oblong leaves 100-180 mm long and 14-30 mm wide, and flowerheads 100-130 mm long and 60-80 mm wide. The lower bracts are papery, cracking and eventually curving backwards like woodshavings; the upper are tipped with a dark fringe and may be pure white, pale pink or deep rosy red, concealing the pale flowers. Occurring in large numbers from Tulbagh discontinuously through to Port Elizabeth along most of the moister coastal mountain chains but, surprisingly, it does not occur on the Klein River mountains. (Feb-Nov)

The similar *P. laurifolia* replaces it on drier inland mountains and may be distinguished by its greyer leaves which have a short but distinct leafstalk, and dark fringed and dark bearded flowers.

Protea speciosa
A many-stemmed, resprouting, fire-resistant shrub to 1,2 m with thick leathery leaves 90-160 mm long and up to 60 mm wide. Plants growing in the Hermanus area have very narrow leaves (10 mm) and were previously thought to be a different species. The oval flowerheads 90-140 mm long are surrounded by pink or cream fringed bracts which almost conceal the flowers. It occurs widely through this area and beyond, from Cape Town to Riversdale as solitary, scattered plants on the mountains between sea level and 1300 m. (June-Jan)

P. stokoei with similar flowers, but always with a single erect stem, occurs in the high mountains from Jonkershoek to Betty's Bay.

Protea compacta   Bot River protea   Botrivier-protea
This stiffly upright, single-stemmed shrub to 3,5 m has its sparse branches largely concealed by the overlapping oblong leaves. The flowerheads are 90-130 mm long with velvety pink bracts overtopping a cone of pink flowers. It occurs in dense stands from near the Palmiet River mouth eastwards to Struisbaai on coastal flats and foothills on sandy soils. (Apr-Sept)

Protea burchellii

Protea neriifolia

Protea speciosa

Protea compacta

PROTEACEAE

Serruria elongata
A shrub with much divided, hairless leaves with cylindrical segments, which are grouped in whorls and confined to the base of the plant. Silver-pink bisexual flowers are borne in clusters grouped towards the top of elongated leafless stalks up to 500 mm long. It is common on the lower and midslopes throughout this area. (Aug-Dec)

Serruria adscendens
An attractive rounded shrub to 1 m with a single main stem and numerous branches. It has finely divided leaves, reddish branches and perfumed silvery pink flowers borne in rounded clusters just above the leaves. It is widespread on flats and lower slopes from Betty's Bay to Bredasdorp and regenerates from seed after veld fires. (Aug-Dec)

The very similar *S. rubricaulis* of the same area differs in being unscented and having many stems, resprouting from the base after fires.

Serruria heterophylla
An erect, single stemmed, sparsely branched shrub to 1 m with hairless leaves up to 60 mm long. The name is derived from the fact that the plant has two different types of leaves. The lower ones are much divided and up to 60 mm long, while the upper ones are much shorter and scarcely dissected. Flowerheads up to 30 mm across are borne in groups on scale-clothed necks, surrounded by 5-10 mm wide membranous bracts. It is quite common on the midslopes from Kleinmond to Hermanus. (Aug-Dec)

The similar, but more brightly coloured *S. rosea* with even broader conspicuous involucral bracts also occurs in this area.

Serruria phylicoides
An erect, rounded, single-stemmed shrub to 600 mm with hairless, finely divided leaves, which give the plant a feathery look. The silver bearded, deep pink to carmine flowers in heads 15 mm in diameter are clustered at the ends of the branches and are surrounded by bracts up to 10 mm long. It may be seen from Houhoek to Bot River, Villiersdorp and Genadendal. (Aug-Dec)

Serruria elongata

Serruria adscendens

Serruria heterophylla

Serruria phylicoides

SANTALACEAE

Thesium carinatum
A yellowish-green, semi-parasitic shrublet to 700 mm with narrow leaves 10 mm long, triangular in cross-section. Clusters of short-stalked sickly sweet scented flowers 2-3 mm long, with bearded sepals, are immersed among leaflike bracts. Occurring on mountain slopes from Clanwilliam to the Cape Peninsula and Caledon, it may bloom at any time of the year.

There are over 300 species in Africa, America and the Old World, of which about 150 occur in Africa, and 27 have been recorded in this area.

Thesium euphorbioides
A distinctive, slender, single-stemmed shrub to 2 m, with a few short branches near the top. The broad, oval, leathery, blue-green leaves enfold the upper stems. The tiny white flowers are borne in clusters among the large bracts at the end of the branches. It occurs on rocky slopes from Tulbagh and Worcester to Stellenbosch, and Caledon to Uitenhage. (Aug-Jan)

GRUBBIACEAE

Grubbia tomentosa
A woody, many-stemmed, branching shrub to 2 m with a fire-resistant stump. The pairs of narrow, open-backed leaves, tapering to both ends, are attached to knobs on the stems. The insignificant flowers, borne in conelike clusters about 5 mm across, give rise to red-purple berries. One of the few fynbos plants with a berry fruit, it occurs scattered on the drier, rocky mountain slopes from Ceres to George. (Dec-Jan)

The 3 species of *Grubbia* which constitute this family all occur in this area. *G. rourkei* of the Kogelberg slopes is single-stemmed; *G. rosmarinifolia* of swamps and stream-sides throughout this area has very narrow leaves, woolly clusters of pink flowers, and hairy wind-dispersed fruits.

BALANOPHORACEAE

Mystropetalon polemannii
A soft perennial plant, wholly parasitic on the roots of members of the Protea family, with annual above ground stems to 250 mm. These consist of a dense spike of unisexual flowers, the females on the lower and males on the upper part. The male flowers have spoon-shaped bracts. It is recorded infrequently from the Malmesbury and Caledon areas, but when it does occur it is found in crowded groups. (Nov-May)

There are 2 species in the southwestern Cape, *M. thomii* differing in having oblong bracts associated with the male flowers.

Theseum carinatum

Theseum euphorbioides

Grubbia tomentosa

Mystropetalon polemannii

AIZOACEAE

Aizoon sarmentosum
A sprawling many stemmed perennial with stems up to 500 mm long, bearing pairs of cylindrical leaves up to 45 mm long. The hairy flowers, about 10 mm across, give rise to woody top-shaped fruits which remain on the older stems for a long period. Occurring on sandy flats and lower slopes from Namaqualand to Swellendam. (June-Oct)

There are about 20 species in the Mediterranean area, Africa and Australia, of which 15 occur in South Africa, but only 1 in this area.

MESEMBRYANTHEMACEAE

This huge largely South African family of about 120 genera and a few thousand species is poorly represented in this area, having perhaps 12 to 14 genera, of which 4 are illustrated here. All species have fleshy leaves, and 'vygie' flowers in all colours except true blue. In all but *Carpobrotus* the seeds are held in tough woody capsules which open when wetted. The genera are identified on the characters of their capsules.

Erepsia inclaudens   Altydvygie
A shrublet to 200 mm with rather weak stems and glossy, translucent-dotted leaves, usually with red tips. The flowers which are held well above the leaves, do not close at night, and are followed by a 5-chambered capsule. It occurs throughout this area on upper mountain slopes and rocky summits. (Aug-Feb)

There are about 20 species occurring in the fynbos region, of which only 3 or 4 have been recorded in this area.

Erepsia anceps
A slender woody shrublet to 500 mm with distant pairs of tapering leaves triangular in cross-section with an outcurving point. The narrow-petalled flowers are about 30 mm across, borne well spaced at the ends of the branches. It is frequent throughout this area and as far east as Danger Point. (Dec-Apr)

Lampranthus furvus   Vygie
A neat rounded shrublet to 250 mm with blue-green leaves 10-15 mm long. The pink to purple flowers are up to 30 mm across, close at night and are followed by 5-chambered capsules. It occurs among rocks on mountain slopes from Clanwilliam and Worcester to the Cape Peninsula and eastwards to Caledon. (Nov-Jan)

There are about 180 species in southern Africa, of which 10 occur in this area. Other pink species are the shrubby estuarine *L. calcaratus*, the mat-forming *L. wordsworthiae*, and the creeping, node-rooting *L. filicaulis*.

Aizoon sarmentosum

Erepsia inclaudens

Erepsia anceps

Lampranthus furvus

MESEMBRYANTHEMACEAE

Lampranthus bicolor
An erect or spreading shrublet, woody at the base, to 500 mm, with brilliant yellow flowers orange on the reverse. This gives the plant a striking two-tone effect. It is common in sand from Tulbagh to the Cape Peninsula and Bredasdorp. (Oct-Dec)

Other yellow-flowered species are the prostrate *L. antemeridianus*, pale rosy beneath; the pure yellow shrubby *L. glaucus;* and the creeping yellow and white *L. reptans*.

Ruschia macowanii
An open mat-forming shrub to 200 mm spreading to 500 mm across or more, but not rooting at the nodes. The hard, fleshy leaves 20-35 mm long by 4 mm thick are joined to form a slight sleeve at the base. The outer petals have a central dark stripe and the paler inner petals and stamens form a cone in the centre. Occurring from Velddrif to Bredasdorp, commonly near the sea. (July-Oct)

There are upwards of 350 species in South Africa, mostly in the drier parts. Others in this area include *R. sarmentosa*, which roots at the nodes; the purplish-pink cushion plant, *R. stokoei*, found at high altitude in the Hottentots Holland and *R. leptophylla* of the coastal forelands with soft leaves and white, pink-flushed flowers.

Carpobrotus edulis Sour fig Suurvy Hotnotsvy
A mat-forming, creeping perennial, rooting at the nodes, with prostrate stems up to 2 m long. The dull green fleshy leaves are triangular in cross-section and 40-80 mm long. The pale yellow flowers fade to pinkish and are followed by fleshy edible fruits. It is usually found in loose sand and is used as an important stabiliser of road verges in the Cape and elsewhere in the world. (Aug-Oct)

There are about 20 species, mainly South African, but also found in Chile and Australia. Three occur in this area.

Carpobrotus acinaciformis Sour fig Hottentots fig Hotnotsvy Suurvy
The prostrate stems are up to 1,5 m long and carry triangular leaves up to 90 mm long and 15-20 mm thick. The brilliant magenta flowers are 120 mm across. It favours loose sand and is found throughout this area at low altitudes. (Aug-Oct)

A third species, the pink to purple-flowered *C. pillansii*, with flowers 65-70 mm across, occurs at high altitudes throughout this area.

Lampranthus bicolor

Ruschia macowanii

Carpobrotus edulis

Carpobrotus acinaciformis

LAURACEAE

Cassytha ciliolata   Devil's sewing thread   Devil's tresses   Nooienshaar
A twining, rootless parasite with yellowish stems approximately the thickness of vermicelli, which attach themselves by means of suckers to the host plant. The sessile, yellowish-white flowers, produced in dense clusters in the axils of the scale-like leaves, give rise to white, red or yellow berries which are eaten by birds. This specimen is parasitising a Grubbia plant. It occurs from Worcester and the Cape Peninsula to the eastern Cape; and may be found in flower and berry at any time of the year.

There are 16 species in the Old World and 2 in South Africa, but only 1 in this area.

RANUNCULACEAE

Anemone tenuifolia   Wild anemone   Syblom
A perennial with stems to 600 mm, and a number of divided, rather hard, dark green leaves 100-200 mm long, with sharply-toothed segments. The hairy pink or white flowers are 80-100 mm across. Occurring on moist slopes from the Hex River mountains and Piketberg to the Cape Peninsula and eastwards to Humansdorp, it blooms most profusely after veld fires. (June-Feb)

A cosmopolitan genus of about 150 species, with 3 in South Africa but only 1 in this area.

BRASSICACEAE

Heliophila linearis var. **reticulata**
A sturdy perennial about 500 mm tall with oval, rather fleshy leaves up to 50 mm by 20 mm. The flowers are typical of the family in having 4 petals in the form of a cross with the 4 sepals peeping out between them. In this variety the flowers are white with very hairy sepals. It occurs in sand and coastal scrub from Malmesbury to the eastern Cape and is common at Vermont near Hermanus. (Aug-Nov)

There are 71 species confined to South Africa of which 14 annuals and 8 perennials occur in this area.

Heliophila macra
A slender, sparsely-branched perennial becoming woody towards the base as it grows to a maximum of 1,3 m, although it is typically much shorter. The undivided, hairless leaves, up to 100 mm by 2 mm are borne mostly near the base of the plant. The pale mauvish, pink or white flowers, up to 23 mm across, are raised high above the leaves and produce erect, flattened, beaked pods with 18-24 seeds. It is frequent on mountain slopes from Caledon to Swellendam. (Oct-Apr)

Cassytha ciliolata

Anemone tenuifolia

Heliophila linearis var. *reticulata*

Heliophila macra

DROSERACEAE

Drosera is a genus of low growing perennials usually found in damp places. The plants derive part of their food requirements from insects which are trapped and digested by the sticky glandular hairs covering the leaves. The delicate flowers wither almost immediately if picked. There are about 125 species worldwide, of which 18 are recorded in South Africa and 8 in this area.

Drosera trinervia   Little sundew

This common yet inconspicuous sundew has a rosette of stalkless leaves, broadest towards the tip, and up to 10 mm long. Up to 10 white (rarely violet) flowers are borne on a leafless stem 50-100 mm high arising from the middle of the leaf rosette. Confined to the southwestern Cape, it flowers especially profusely after veld fires. (Aug-Nov)

Two other rosette-forming species occur in this area: *D. acaulis* with single red or purple flowers nestling among the leaves; and *D. aliciae* with a spike of purple flowers borne on a stem emerging from the side of the rosette.

Drosera hilaris   Sprawling sundew

Very deep-rooted with an unbranched leafy stem to 250 mm high. The leaves are up to 70 mm long. The flowers, up to 20 mm across, only open in sunlight. It is found on sheltered mountain slopes from the Cape Peninsula to Hermanus. (Sept-Nov)

Drosera cistiflora   Sundew Doublom

A soft weakly erect perennial with an unbranched stem to 200 mm high. The leaves are 20-30 mm long. The white or rose flowers have a dark green eye. Found on sandy, often well-drained slopes or temporary seepages from Namaqualand to Port Elizabeth. (Aug-Sept)

Three other sundews have leafy stems. *D. ramentacea* has a branched stem; *D. capensis* has leaves up to 150 mm long with a well-defined leafstalk; and *D. glabripes* has long erect hairs clothing the stem between the leaves.

RORIDULACEAE

Roridula gorgonias   Vlieëbos

This plant is related to the *Droseras*. It is a woody, sparingly-branched shrublet to 1 m or more. The narrow leaves, up to 120 mm long are crowded at the tips of the branches and are covered with sticky immovable tentacles. The pink flowers are 20 mm across. It occurs in scattered colonies in damp places on the mountains from Somerset West to Swellendam. (July-Oct)

There are 2 species in South Africa, both endemic to the Cape fynbos, but this is the only 1 in this area.

Drosera trinervia

Drosera hilaris

Drosera cistiflora

Roridula gorgonias

CRASSULACEAE

Cotyledon orbiculata   Pig's ear   Varksoor   Kouteri
A shrub to 1 m with thick, fleshy branches and pairs of thick, waxy, green or grey leaves often with red edges, 50-100 mm long by 20-50 mm wide, widest in the upper third. The waxy red or pinkish flowers are up to 25 mm long. Occurring widely in Namibia and South Africa and said to be poisonous, it may flower throughout the year.

It is the only species in this area. There are about 150 species in Africa, Asia, Mexico and Europe, of which about 10 occur in the Cape Province.

Crassula fascicularis   Klipblom
A more or less branched succulent perennial with stems up to 400 mm high bearing pointed, slightly fleshy leaves which are often hairy-edged. The jasmine-like flowers have petals up to 32 mm long, white to pale cream or green, sometimes pink-tinged, which do not broaden towards the tips. It occurs from Vanrhynsdorp to Bredasdorp on lower fynbos slopes and is sweetly-scented in the evening. (Sept-Nov)

There are about 300 species, mainly in Africa and India, with perhaps 30 in this area. Another large-flowered species is *C. obtusa* of mountain rock pools with narrow fleshy leaves and pale petals, flushed red, which broaden towards the tips.

Adromischus caryophyllaceus   Nentabos
A branched succulent shrublet with tough, uniformly green, spoon-shaped or oval leaves 25-40 mm by 10-20 mm with rounded edges. The flowers, borne in spikes on stems up to 200 mm long are about 20 mm long with petals joined to form a tube concealing the stamens. It is found on the coastal plain from Hermanus to Mossel Bay and inland areas of the Caledon district to Uniondale. (Oct-Mar)

There are 26 species in South Africa with 2 in this area; *A. hemisphaericus* differs in having protruding anthers and spotted leaves.

Crassula coccinea   Red Crassula   Klipblom
A succulent shrublet to 600 mm with thick branches, but seldom as robust as the specimen illustrated. It has overlapping, thinly fleshy, hairy-edged leaves 12-25 mm by 10-15 mm. The brilliant red (rarely white) flowers have 5 petals joined into a tube near the base. It is common in rock crevices and on ledges on sandstone from the Cape Peninsula to Bredasdorp. (Dec-Jan)

Cotyledon orbiculata

Crassula fascicularis

Adromischus caryophyllaceus

Crassula coccinea

BRUNIACEAE

Berzelia and **Brunia** are 2 closely related genera, distinguished by the fact that *Berzelias* have a single style, whilst *Brunias* have 2. This feature cannot be seen with the naked eye. All species have their flowers closely packed into dense rounded heads, which remain on the plant for a year or more.

Berzelia incurva   Klipknopbossie

A much-branched shrub to 1 m with crowded, incurved, hairy-edged leaves 6-7 mm long. The flower heads are 6-7 mm across and occur in groups of 1-3 on short twiglets near the tips of the branches. It is uncommon and confined to rocky upper slopes in the east of this area. (Jan-Mar)

There are 12 species, endemic to the south and southwestern Cape, of which 7 occur in this area. *B. ecklonii*, found in the west of this area, has shorter leaves (4-5 mm) with flowerheads 10 mm across, borne singly at the tips of erect branchlets and grouped to form a compound head.

Berzelia squarrosa   Spiderbush

A resprouting erect shrub to 1,5 m with spreading leaves 10-15 mm long and 1-2 mm wide. Each flowerhead is 6-8 mm across, growing singly on a short stalk and grouped to form a flattish compound head at the ends of the branches. It occurs in marshy areas and streamsides throughout this area. (Aug-Sept)

Other species include the leggy *B. rubra* of the Klein River mountains with flowerheads borne on short shoots in small groups up the stem, and the common *B. lanuginosa*, 'kolkol', with 0,5 mm wide feathery leaves and 5 mm wide cream flowerheads.

Brunia alopecuroides

A sturdy erect shrub about 1,5 m tall with crowded, hairless leaves about 4 mm long covering the numerous slender branchlets. The flowerheads are about 5 mm across and are borne in short spikes on pale flowering stems, which are grouped into large heads 150 mm or more across at the ends of the main branches. It forms dense stands in marshy areas on mountain slopes throughout this area. (Sept-Jan)

There are about 7 species confined to the fynbos area of South Africa, of which 6 occur in this area.

Brunia alopecuroides

The fruit of this species is far more distinctive than the flower. As the flowers fade the hard fruiting heads turn deep red. The tip of the plant grows on to produce the next season's flowers, leaving the fruits clustered among the leaves like miniature berries. They gradually fade to brown and may remain on the plant for a further season, some being just visible at the bottom of the illustration.

Berzelia incurva

Berzelia squarrosa

Brunia alopecuroides

Brunia alopecuroides (fruit)

BRUNIACEAE

Staavia radiata   Altydbossie
An open shrublet with numerous short slender branches to 800 mm, sprouting from a fire-resistant stump. It bears fairly crowded pointed leaves 4-7 mm long, and daisy-like flowerheads 6-8 mm across, either singly or in groups. Occurring at low to moderate altitudes on sandy flats and slopes from Malmesbury to Bredasdorp and on to Knysna. It blooms all year round.

There are 9 species endemic to the fynbos areas of South Africa, of which 2 more may be found in this area. The sturdy *S. brownii* is quite common on coastal slopes near the mouth of the Steenbras River, and has whitish flowers perhaps 15 mm across. *S. capitella* is recorded from Houhoek and the Klein River mountains, having pale flowers 12 mm across and round-tipped leaves.

Brunia laevis
A rounded shrub to 900 mm with needlelike grey overlapping slightly hairy leaves. The long-stemmed cream flowerheads, each 15 mm across, form shallow clusters and are supported below by a sturdy very hairy collar of bracts. It occurs on hills and lower mountain slopes from Houhoek to Bredasdorp. (Aug-Jan)

Brunia neglecta is very similar, but the leaves become hairless.

Brunia albiflora   Coffee bush
A shrub to 3 m with many side branches conspicuously more slender than the main axis, and several flushes of flowerheads persisting on the plant. The crowded spreading very thin leaves are up to 12 mm long and the flowerheads, borne singly on stalks about 40 mm long, are up to 15 mm across and form a flat-topped group. It usually occurs in dense stands in rather damp places on the Klein River and Hottentots Holland mountains, and emits an elusive coffee scent. (Mar-Apr)

Pseudobaeckia africana   Streambush
A dainty slender branched shrub to 3 m with hairy branchlets and needlelike leaves 10-35 mm long. The flowers, in short spikes, are crowded in clusters between the leaves. Occurring on mountain slopes near streams, and on the edges of mountain pools from Clanwilliam to Caledon. (Sept-Nov)

There are 4 species confined to the fynbos areas of South Africa, of which 3 occur in this area. The other 2 have broad leaves: *P. cordata* has dense spheres of flowers, 2-5 mm across, at the tips of branches; the flowers of *P. stokoei* nestle in the axils of the crowded, overlapping hairy leaves.

Staavia radiata

Brunia laevis

Brunia albiflora

Pseudobaeckia africana

BRUNIACEAE

Raspalia microphylla False cedar
A much branched shrub to 900 mm, with crowded, smooth round-backed scale-like leaves up to 1,8 mm long, with a minute stumpy black tip. The single terminal whitish flowerheads are 3-4 mm across. It grows on rocky outcrops at high altitudes from Paarl to Bredasdorp and Swellendam. (Sept-Jan)
There are 16 species, mainly in the southwestern Cape, of which 5 occur in this area, none of them common. Three more have tiny scale-like leaves and whitish flowers. The leaves of *R. virgata* are smooth but have a ridge down the back; the leaves of *R. variabilis* and *R. phylicoides* are hairy, the former with a ridge, the latter round-backed; *R. globosa* has broader leaves and magenta flowers.

Brunia stokoei Rooistompie
An erect rigid shrub 1-2 m high with hairless needlelike leaves 8-10 mm long. It is the only species with red flowers, borne in heads about 15 mm across, with very imperfectly developed collars of bracts below. The flowerheads illustrated are only partly open. Occurring on the lower mountain slopes in the Kleinmond and Betty's Bay areas. (Nov-Apr)

Nebelia paleacea Bergstompie
A dense rounded much-branched shrub to 1 m or more, resprouting from a fire-resistant stump after veld fires. The leaves are 3-6 mm long, almost without hairs, and held close to the twig. The flowerheads, immersed in long spiky bracts, are up to 7 mm across, and borne upon branched shoots at the top of the main stem. Occurring in a diversity of soils and aspects from sea level to middle altitudes from Clanwilliam to Riversdale. (Mainly Oct-Feb)
There are 6 species of which 2 others occur in this area. The more erect, *N. fragarioides* has round compound flowerheads about 8 mm across, crowded into dense heads perhaps 20-30 mm across, which in bud have a lumpy appearance. The high altitude *N. sphaerocephala* is a massive hairy shrub with individual heads 20-30 mm across, not collected into groups.

Brunia nodiflora Stompie Fonteinbossie Volstruisies
A shrub to 900 mm resprouting from a persistent stump after veld fires. The fairly hairy branches are closely covered with sessile leaves 2-3 mm long. The cream flowerheads with their long stamens have a fluffier appearance than any other species. They are 10 mm across and supported below by a sturdy collar of tightly packed hairy bracts. Common on hills and mountain slopes from Piketberg to Uitenhage. (Mar-June)

Raspalia microphylla

Brunia stokoei

Nebelia paleacea

Brunia nodiflora

ROSACEAE

Cliffortia ruscifolia Climber's friend Steekbos
A much-branched, spiny shrub to 1,5 m or more with very hairy young growths and lance-shaped leaves, spine-tipped and 10-20 mm long, each with 2 small pointed stipules tucked between leaf and twig. The wind-pollinated male and female flowers are almost always borne on separate plants. They have a calyx of 3 lobes and no petals. The female (illustrated here) has a long feathery stigma projecting well beyond the leaves, and the male a group of projecting stamens. Common among rocks from Namaqualand to Humansdorp. The common name "Climber's friend" refers to its reliability as a holdfast in rock crevices for it is exceedingly firmly rooted, and not ironically, to its extremely prickly nature. (Aug-Oct)

There are about 108 species confined chiefly to South Africa of which 35 occur in this area. The very similar *C. multiformis* of the Klein River mountains differs in having hairless leaves.

FABACEAE

Argyrolobium lunare
A silvery weak-stemmed shrublet often sprawling through other plants, with compound pinnate leaves. Long-stalked clusters of bright yellow flowers, each 15 mm long, are borne well above the leaves, and age to a rich reddish-brown. Fairly common on lower slopes from Clanwilliam to the Riviersonderend mountains. (Sept-Dec)

There are about 150 species in Africa, the Mediterranean and India, of which only 1 other occurs here: *A. filiforme* is a dwarf tufted perennial resprouting after veld fires.

Aspalathus crenata
An erect or sprawling rather sparsely-branched shrub to 1,5 m with sharply angled and winged branches, bearing oval, spine-tipped, simple leaves. The flowers have a silky reverse. It is found on lower slopes from Clanwilliam to Caledon, including Jonkershoek, Hangklip and Houhoek. (Sept-Dec)

There are about 255 species in South Africa, mainly in the Cape, of which some 94 occur in this area.

Cyclopia genistoides Honey tea Heuningtee
A dense rounded almost hairless shrub to 700 mm, with trifoliate leaves, the leaflets having rolled-back edges and bearing clusters of bright yellow 10-15 mm long flowers. Widespread on flats and slopes throughout this area and extending eastward to Uniondale. A pleasant tea can be made of the young twigs. (July-Dec)

There are 20 species confined to South Africa, of which 2 others occur in this area: *C. maculata* is found beside streams on lower slopes; *C. falcata*, with broad flat leaves occurs on upper slopes in the northwest of this area.

Cliffortia ruscifolia

Argyrolobium lunare

Aspalathus crenata

Cyclopia genistoides

FABACEAE

Aspalathus excelsa
An erect, much-branched relatively short-lived shrub or small tree to 2,5 m with tufts of narrow fleshy hairless leaves, 6-15 mm long. Groups of 5-15 bright yellow sweetly-scented flowers up to 12 mm long are borne on short, hairy stalks. It is abundant in the first decade after a veld fire and occurs on sandy lowlands at the foot of the Klein River mountains near the coast. (Sept-Nov)

Aspalathus laricifolia ssp. **laricifolia**
A prostrate, usually sparsely-branched shrublet to 500 mm with needlelike, non-spiny leaves 3-12 mm long. Light to bright yellow flowers are borne in open groups towards the ends of the stems. Occurring in sand on lower mountain slopes, and also on limestone from Tulbagh and Worcester to George. (Sept-Dec)

Aspalathus ciliaris
A variable, erect or spreading shrub to 1,5 m, arising from a fire-resistant stump. It has woolly stems and tufts of up to 20 trifoliate leaves, which appear spiky but are in fact soft to the touch and are covered with long hairs. Clusters of bright yellow flowers, densely hairy on the reverse, are borne on lateral branchlets. Common on sandy, clayey or limestone flats and hills and lower mountain slopes from the Cedarberg and Saldanha Bay to Humansdorp. (Oct-Jan)

Liparia splendens   Mountain dahlia   Orange nodding head
                                       Klipblom   Skaamblom
An almost hairless, spreading shrub to 1 m, sometimes dense and rounded, with oval leaves 30-50 mm long. The swordlike leaves in the illustration are misleading as they do not belong to this plant, but a few of its own leaves can be seen on the pale stem in the lower centre of the photograph. Numerous flowers are crowded into globose heads 60-80 mm across at the ends of the branches. Occurring on rocky mountain slopes from Paarl and the Cape Peninsula to Mossel Bay, it can bloom at any time of the year.

There are 2 species confined to the Cape but this is the only 1 in this area.

Aspalathus excelsa

Aspalathus laricifolia ssp. *laricifolia*

Aspalathus ciliaris

Liparia splendens

FABACEAE

Indigofera mauritanica Sprawling pea
A much-branched straggling, hairy shrub, becoming hairless and distinctly woody at the base. The leaves are divided into 5-7 variable leaflets up to 10 mm long, but more often half that, on a very short stalk. The long-stalked heads of rose to purple flowers are followed by dark, hairy pods. Occurring on sandy flats and slopes from the Cape Peninsula to Caledon, it blooms throughout the year.

There are 750 species in the warmer parts of the world of which 15 occur in this area. The similar *I. sarmentosa* has many trailing branches at ground level, and smaller leaves.

Indigofera filifolia Leafless pea
An erect, hairless, seemingly leafless shrub to 2 m. A few pinnate leaves do occur but fall off very young, leaving only the 75-125 mm long stalk. The rose to purple flowers are borne in loose racemes at the ends of the long stems. It is found at streamsides from the Gifberg and Cape Peninsula to George. (Dec-Apr)

Hypocalyptus coluteoides Rooikeur
A lanky, highly ornamental shrub to 3 m with hairy young branches and almost hairless, blueish-green, trifoliate leaves with leaflets widest in the middle. The crowded elongated clusters of purple to bright pink flowers have sepals all the same size, but with the top 2 cut straight across the tips. Several seeds are produced in a hairless pod. Occurring at forest edges and along streams from Caledon to Humansdorp. (July-Nov)

There are 3 species confined to the southwestern Cape, all of which occur in this area: the similar *H. sophoroides*, a robust shrub to 4 m, with leaflets widest at the tips may be seen in the northwest of the area; the third species, *H. oxalidifolius* is unlike the others, being a thin-stemmed sprawling shrublet with dainty sprays of pale pink flowers.

Podalyria calyptrata Pink keurtjie Keurblom Ertjieblom
A stout, moderately-branched silvery silky shrub to 3 m, with simple leaves 20-50 mm long. They have a slight projection at the tip and the side-veins are clearly visible. The pink (occasionally white), sweetly-scented flowers are borne 2 per stalk in the axils of the leaves; they are followed by hairy, inflated pods, holding several seeds. The bracts form a unique hood or cap, which breaks away as the bud swells to reveal the hairy calyx. Occurring in ravines or on moist hillsides at low and mid-altitudes, with a dwarf form on rocks near the sea, from the Cape Peninsula to Bredasdorp. (Aug-Oct)

Indigofera mauritanica

Indigofera filifolia

Hypocalyptus coluteoides

Podalyria calyptrata

FABACEAE

Otholobium obliquum
An erect shrub to 1,2 m bearing gland-dotted, crowded leaves each with 3 hair-tipped leaflets 22-34 mm by 6-8 mm in size. The lateral leaflets are very lop-sided. The pale blue flowers nestle among the leaves on rather short stalks, and are followed by 1-seeded pods. Scattered plants occur on the mountain slopes at Paarl, Stellenbosch and Caledon. (July-Nov)
 There are 40 species in Africa, of which 4 may occur in this area.

Priestleya vestita
A sturdy sparsely-branched shrub to 2 m, with densely-hairy silvery branches and broad, almost square, overlapping leaves which are sparsely-bristled above amd shaggy below. The short-stalked flowers are arranged in compact terminal heads, and turn brown with age. Occurring on moist mountain slopes, it is especially showy for a few seasons after a veld fire. (May-Feb)
 There are 18 species in the southwest Cape, of which about 12 may occur in this area; the only similar species, *P. calycina* differs in the leaves being longer than broad and more pointed.

Rafnia cuneifolia
An entirely hairless, often sprawling shrub to 1 m, blackening when bruised or dead, with simple, smooth-edged, oval leaves. The short-stalked flowers, borne in the axils of the leaves, are about 12 mm long, with a calyx of 5 lobes, the lowest much narrower than the rest. Occurring on mountain slopes from Ceres and Tulbagh to Caledon. (Oct-Feb)
 There are about 22 species in South Africa from the Cape to Natal, of which 9 have been recorded from this area.

Lebeckia simsiana
A shrub with rather weak, branched stems to 600 mm and needlelike, 10-12 mm long grey-green leaves, with a joint above the middle. The short-stalked yellow flowers arise at the ends of branches in the axils of minute bristle-like bracts. Each flower is 15 mm long. Occasional plants are found from Clanwilliam to Swellendam. (Sept-Jan)
 There are 45 species in South Africa and Madagascar, of which 4 may occur in this area: *L. grandiflora* also has jointed leaves, with bracts as long as the flowerstalks; *L. pauciflora* has bracts half as long or less, and leaves without joints and *L. wrightii* has single orange-yellow flowers in the axils of the leaves.

Otholobium obliquum

Priestleya vestita

Rafnia cuneifolia

Lebeckia simsiana

FABACEAE

Psoralea aphylla　　　　　　　　　　　　　　Fonteinbos　Bloukeur
A slender hairy shrub 1-3 m tall with apparently leafless branches which arch downwards under the weight of the flowers. The scale-like leaves are 3-6 mm long, and the sweetly scented flowers are borne on stalks clothed with black hairs. It is found in marshes and along streams from Clanwilliam to Worcester and the Cape Peninsula to Riversdale. (Oct-Feb)
　　There are 130 species worldwide of which 50 occur in Africa and 11 in this area. They are sprinkled with small dark or translucent dots.

Psoralea pinnata　　　　　　　　　　Fonteinbos　Bloukeur　Penwortel
An erect shrub or small tree to 4 m with rather willowy branches. Each compound leaf bears 7-11 needle-like leaflets 20-30 mm long. The lilac-blue and white sweetly-scented flowers are grouped in axillary clusters towards the ends of the branchlets. It occurs in wet places from Clanwilliam to the eastern Cape and Transvaal and may flower at any time of the year.

Rhynchosia ferulifolia
A prostrate, slender, almost hairless shrub with many stems to 1 m long. The leaves are variably complex-compound from the simplest 3-leaflet condition as seen in the illustration, to many leaflets. The dense clusters of sticky yellow flowers on 50-150 mm stalks, and the leaves and calyx are gland-dotted. Found on sandy flats from Piketberg and the Cape Peninsula to Knysna. (July-Jan)
　　There are 300 species, cosmopolitan in the warmer parts of the world, of which 5 occur in this area.

Tephrosia capensis　　　　　　　　　　　　　　　　　　　Fish bean
A trailing, straggly perennial with sparse compound leaves on 20 mm long stalks, each consisting of 3-6 pairs of oval leaflets some 20 mm long with a pointed tip. The sparse pink to rose-red flowers are followed by straight, opaque, hairy pods with numerous seeds. It occurs from the coastal dunes to the high mountain slopes, on any kind of soil, from the Cape Peninsula to the eastern Cape and Transvaal. (July-Apr)
　　There are about 400 species pan-tropical and sub-tropical, but this is the only one in this area.

Psoralea aphylla *Psoralea pinnata*

Rhynchosia ferulifolia *Tephrosia capensis*

GERANIACEAE

Erodium incarnatum Crane's bill Horlosies Vrouebossie
A sprawling perennial to 250 mm with rough, much-divided upper leaves and heart-shaped, lobed, lower leaves. The distinctively marked flowers have 5 fertile and 5 infertile stamens and are 20 mm across. Occurring on stony hillsides in the Caledon, Worcester and Robertson districts, usually in thick undergrowth or under bushes. (Aug-Nov)
  There are 50 species worldwide in temperate regions with 5 occurring in this area, the others being introduced weeds of disturbed places.

Pelargonium cucullatum Tree pelargonium Wilde malva
A sturdy hairy shrub to 2 m or more, woody at the base but with sappy new growth. The kidney-shaped aromatic, 45 mm long leaves are cupped and pleated with irregular, sometimes reddish edges. The hollow-stalked flowers are usually pink to purple, but a white form is sometimes found. The bright orange pollen on the 7 fertile stamens is usually conspicuous. This form occurs on coastal flats and lower slopes from Gordon's Bay to Gansbaai and in the Cape Peninsula. A subspecies, *P. cucullatum* ssp. *strigifolium*, differing only in the leaves being of a harsher texture, is found further inland and at higher altitudes than the typical form. (Sept-Feb)
  There are 250 species in Africa and the middle east, with some 40 in this area.

Pelargonium myrrhifolium
A soft hairy shrublet to 400 mm with weak stems bearing very deeply divided leaves about 80 mm long, including the long leafstalk. Up to 4 white or pale pink flowers are carried well above the leaves. The upper petals are much larger than the lower and have carmine nectar guides. Found mostly on sandy soil, it is common from Clanwilliam to Willowmore and blooms throughout the year.

OXALIDACEAE

The sorrels, a group of about 500 species, mainly in Africa but also in America, with some 26 in this area. They are among the very few dicotyledons with bulbs. The sepals and leaves may have tiny patches of coloured and slightly thickened tissue, known as callusses, towards the tips.

Oxalis dentata
A delicate unbranched plant to 300 mm with leaves on 20-60 mm stalks. Each leaf has 3 drooping partly bi-lobed leaflets up to 9 mm long. Clusters of rosy, violet or pink flowers, often appearing before the leaves, are raised high above them on a partly-hairy stem. It occurs in dense stands in damp shady places under other plants, from the Cape Peninsula to Caledon. (Mar-May)

Erodium incarnatum

Pelargonium cucullatum

Pelargonium myrrhifolium

Oxalis dentata

OXALIDACEAE

Oxalis polyphylla
Vingersuring

An erect plant up to 300 mm high with many unbranched stems produced from a compound bulb, and leaves and flowers attached in a dense tuft at the top. The slightly hairy leaf-stalks are 10-50 mm long, and bear 3-7 slender parallel-sided leaflets 10-30 mm long, folded lengthwise. The rosy-pink, purple or white flowers are 15-30 mm long, often with dark-edged petals and are borne on long stalks arising singly between the leaves. The hairy sepals have 2 orange dots at the tips. Occurring in all kinds of soil from Ceres to Port Elizabeth. (Mar-June)

Oxalis purpurea
Stemless, with a few leaves at ground level, each divided into 3 rounded leaflets. They are hairless above, but hairy and sometimes purple below, often with a visible fringe of white hairs around the edge, and liberally sprinkled with minute translucent dots and streaks, barely visible to the unaided eye, which blacken on drying. The single flower may be violet, rose, salmon or white on a short stem which has 2 small bracts towards the base. Widespread from Namaqualand to Caledon at low altitude. (Apr-Sept)

Oxalis luteola
A stemless, hairy, or smooth dwarf to 80 mm. The leaves, with stalks up to 40 mm long, are divided into 3 rounded leaflets, each with a shallow indentation at the tip. The yellow flowers are borne singly on stalks which, after flowering, arch over to bring the developing seeds near to the ground. Occurring in sandy soil on flats and lower mountain slopes from Clanwilliam to Riversdale, it is the only yellow-flowered species in this area with a ground-hugging rosette of leaves. (May-Aug)

The diminutive yellow-flowered *O. corniculata*, whose flowers are 7 mm long, is a creeping, rooting, cosmopolitan weed.

Oxalis tenuifolia
A slender plant with more or less hairy stems to 240 mm tall, and small tufts of leaves along the length of the stem, with a larger tuft at the tip. The nearly sessile leaves are divided into 3 up-folded, very narrow, hairy leaflets 4-9 mm long. The abundant white flowers, borne singly on hairy stalks, have hairy petals 10-25 mm long with a striking purple edge. A common species of shady places from Paarl to Caledon, it blooms in the cooler months. (May-Aug)

O. multicaulis is similar with stalkless leaves and white, purple-edged petals, but it has several long orange patches on the sepals.

Oxalis polyphylla

Oxalis purpurea

Oxalis luteola

Oxalis tenuifolia

OXALIDACEAE

Oxalis truncatula
A tufted, stemless or short-stemmed, densely-silky plant with thick firm-textured dark-green leaves, often purple below, on stalks 10-60 mm long. Each leaf has 3 leaflets increasing greatly in size after flowering, to 40 mm across. The solitary hairy flowers, 14-24 mm long, are borne on delicate stalks and are produced rather ahead of the leaves. Scattered on mountain slopes and quite common in hard stony ground from Paarl and Caledon to Bredasdorp. (Apr-June)

Oxalis eckloniana
A stemless, dwarf plant with hairy leafstalks, bearing 3 rounded leaflets, hairy on mid-rib and edge, and green or purple below. The flowers are 15-35 mm long, with narrow-pointed shaggy sepals, and are borne on hairy stalks up to 100 mm long, which curve downwards when the flowers fade. When the flower is opened up, the stamens spring outwards. A variable species, widespread from Clanwilliam to Mossel Bay. (Apr-June)

LINACEAE

Linum africanum Cape flax
A soft hairless perennial to 500 mm with long narrow leaves mostly in pairs. A dark gland is visible on either side of the point of attachment of each leaf. The 10-15 mm long petals drop off very easily, and the styles are joined together for less than half their length. Occurring in a wide variety of habitats at low altitudes in sand or limestone, usually near the coast, from Worcester and the Cape Peninsula to Knysna. (Nov-Jan)

There are about 230 species world-wide, and 14 in South Africa, all yellow-flowered, of which 7 have been recorded in this area. *L. quadrifolium* of low mid-altitudes, is the only species with leaves in whorls of 4; *L. thunbergii* has glands on most of the lower, sometimes 4-whorled leaves.

ZYGOPHYLLACEAE

Zygophyllum sessilifolium
A slender prostrate shrub forming clumps about 750 mm across, with soft branches bearing pairs of oval, harsh-edged, sharp-pointed, sessile leaves. The white or yellow, usually purple-streaked flowers, are borne on stalks longer than the leaves, and have pointed green sepals. Occurring on sandy flats and lower slopes from Clanwilliam to the Cape Peninsula and east perhaps as far as George. (Apr-Oct)

There are about 100 species in Africa and Australia, of which half occur in South Africa, with 3 in this area. *Z. flexuosum* is a tall shrub with broad blunt yellow-brown sepals; and the straggling *Z. fulvum* has pointed red sepals.

Oxalis truncatula

Oxalis eckloniana

Linum africanum

Zygophyllum sessilifolium

RUTACEAE

In this family the leaves are dotted with small oil glands, which, when crushed, emit a powerful scent, often so characteristic that the species may be identified by it. In this area all are shrubs. The flowers have 5 petals and stamens, and a 2-5 chambered fruit, usually with a horn at the top of each chamber.

Adenandra acuta
An ascending shrublet to 600 mm with narrow, leathery, lance-shaped leaves 6-9 mm long with unthickened edges. The short-stalked flowers have narrow long-tapered sepals. The petals are tipped with a reddish knob. Occurring at fairly high altitudes from Grabouw to Franschhoek. (Oct-Dec)

There are 18 species confined to the fynbos area of the Cape, of which 9 have been recorded in this area. *A. villosa* also has short-stalked flowers in compact clusters, but lacks the reddish knob on the petals.

Adenandra viscida
A branched shrublet to 500 mm resprouting from a persistent stump after veld fires. The sparsely gland-dotted 6-12 mm long leaves are pale beneath with a green midrib and thick edges. The almost sessile flowers are grouped in gummy heads and have long non-hairy stalks with broad blunt-tipped purple-spotted sepals. The 8-12 mm long petals have a pinkish reverse. Occurring on rocky hillsides or in coastal fynbos from Onrus east to Bredasdorp. (Aug-Dec)

It is known to hybridise with *A. brachyphylla*. No other *Adenandras* in this area have sticky flowerheads.

Adenandra brachyphylla
A lanky, moderately-branched shrublet to 800 mm resprouting from a persistent stump after veld fires, with tiny heart-shaped leaves. The flowers are in clusters of 2-4 on long non-hairy stalks at the branch tips. The sepals are broad, blunt-tipped, often purple-spotted, with 9-12 mm long petals, notched at the tip, with a red reverse. Common on rocky slopes from Houhoek south and east to the Klein River mountains. (July-Nov)

Four other species have flowers on measurable stalks, including the small-flowered *A. multiflora* of the Houhoek area, and *A. lasiantha* of the Klein River mountains, with its very hairy flowerstalks 4-18 mm long.

Agathosma juniperifolia   Stream buchu
A tall, elegant shrub to 2,5 m with arching branches and needlelike leaves to 10 mm long. The open clusters of long-stalked flowers with short-stalked petals and threadlike sterile stamens, are borne on branch-tips and are followed by horned 2-chambered capsules. Occurring near streams from the Cedarberg and Jonkershoek to the Riviersonderend mountains. (June-Dec)

There are about 145 species in South Africa of which 14 occur in this area.

Adenandra acuta

Adenandra viscida

Adenandra brachyphylla

Agathosma juniperifolia

POLYGALACEAE

Muraltia ericoides
An erect or spreading shrublet to 400 mm with hairy young stems, often branching at ground level. The leaves are sharp-pointed, 4-12 mm long with hairy margins when young. The pink and magenta flowers have a pleated horizontal frill projecting from the mouth. Found on flats and lower mountain slopes from Malmesbury to Uniondale. (Aug-Apr)

This is one of a group of about 115 species of small, often prickly, shrublets of which 24 have been recorded in this area.

Polygala This is a genus characterised by having 2 of its 5 sepals much enlarged and brightly coloured so as to resemble petals. There are 3 petals, the lowest of which has a crest rather like a shaving brush. There are about 600 species worldwide, of which approximately 86 occur in southern Africa, and 11 in this area.

Polygala bracteolata
A lax or erect perennial to 800 mm, branching mostly at the base, with lance-shaped narrow leaves up to 30 mm long. The pink, magenta or rarely white, 12-19 mm long flowers, borne in crowded clusters at the ends of the main branches, have a white crest. Recorded from Vanrhynsdorp to Humansdorp and throughout this area from sea level to 900 m. (Aug-Nov)

Polygala umbellata
A lax or erect perennial to 400 mm, branching mainly near the woody base, with needle-like leaves up to 18 mm long. The crowded clusters of slender-stalked pink or magenta flowers are usually less than 11 mm long and the 2 large side sepal lobes almost conceal the petals and purple crest within. Occurring on dry, lower, often rocky slopes from Ceres to Riversdale. (Aug-Oct)

Two similar species with narrow leaves are *P. meridionalis*, of limey coastal sands and *P. garcini* with white-crested flowers arranged in tapering loose racemes.

Polygala myrtifolia   Blou-ertjieblom   Septemberbossie
A sturdy much-branched shrub to 2 m with variable bright green leaves and magenta, pink or occasionally white, pale-crested flowers up to 22 mm long, in short terminal racemes. Occurring in coastal scrub, forest margins or river valleys from Vanrhynsdorp to the Transkei, and Bredasdorp to the Swartberg; it is not confined to the fynbos. A variable, adaptable and widely cultivated shrub, it blooms at any time of the year.

Muraltia ericoides

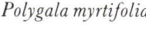

Polygala bracteolata

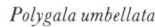

Polygala umbellata

Polygala myrtifolia

EUPHORBIACEAE

Clutia polygonoides
A hairless shrublet to 600 mm with many sparsely branched stems coppicing from a fire-resistant rootstock. The leathery leaves are narrow, oblong and 12-18 mm long. The flowers are yellow or orange, about 4 mm long, with males and females on separate plants. The male flowers are borne in clusters, whilst the female flowers are solitary and followed by round hairless capsules. Occurring on the upper mountain slopes from Clanwilliam to Riversdale. There are about 70 species in Africa of which 9 occur in this area. (June-Oct)

Euphorbia silenifolia Melkbol
A dwarf, tuberous geophyte to 75 mm with annual leaves and flowering stems. The male and female flowers are borne in clusters on separate plants. Occurring at upper altitudes from Ceres to Grahamstown. (Apr-Nov)
   This is a huge genus of over 2000 species worldwide, with about 200 in South Africa, and 7 in this area. All exude a milky sap when damaged. Two of these are succulents and the other 5 non-succulents. The very similar *E. tuberosa* occurs at lower altitudes and differs in having broader, more spreading leaves.

Euphorbia erythrina Pisgoed
A perennial sparsely-branched hairless shrublet to 700 mm with crowded narrow leaves. The flowerhead stalks may be branched, and arise from a circle of leaves. The capsule is rounded and 3-chambered. Occurring from Ceres and the Cape Peninsula to the eastern Cape. (June-Oct)
   E. foliosa is similar, but half the size in most respects.

Clutia rubricaulis Jeukbossie
A hairless shrub to 700 mm with sessile oval, blunt-tipped leaves with a fine point at the tip, and a flat, very fine-toothed edge. The cream-coloured 4 mm long flowers of the male, shown here, are borne in clusters which emerge beyond the leaves. The female produces round hairless capsules. Occurring on coastal flats or lower slopes from Namaqualand to Paarl and through to Port Elizabeth. (June-Feb)
   The similar *C. alaternoides* has leaves with smooth translucent edges; *C. pubescens* has hairy branches and capsules.

Clutia polygonoides

Euphorbia silenifolia

Euphorbia erythrina

Clutia rubricaulis

ANACARDIACEAE

Rhus laevigata   Dune taaibos
An untidy, often deciduous, much-branched shrub to 2 m, the branches often infested with pea-sized galls. The leaves may be hairy or smooth, and are divided into 3 leaflets, the middle one largest at about 40 mm by 25 mm. The net-veins are translucent when held up to the light. The insignificant flowers are unisexual, borne on separate bushes. It occurs on the coastal plain and lower foothills from Lambert's Bay to the eastern Cape. (Aug-Mar)

There are about 250 species worldwide in the subtropics and temperate regions and over 60 in South Africa, of which 9 occur in this area.

Laurophyllus capensis   Iron martin   Ystermartiens
A resinous, densely leafy, evergreen shrub or small tree to 6 m, with oblong leathery leaves. The male and female flowers are borne on separate plants. The female (represented here) has small white flowers within overlapping, woody, coarsely-fringed bracts, which turn brown and remain on the plant for a number of seasons. The numerous tiny male flowers are borne loosely at the ends of the branches. It is recorded from streamsides in coastal forest from the Hottentots Holland to Uitenhage, and is the only species. (Aug-Jan)

CELASTRACEAE

Pterocelastrus tricuspidatus   Cherrywood   Kershout
A shrub or small tree to 7 m or occasionally more with alternate, leathery blunt-tipped leaves 30-80 mm long by 10-40 mm wide, and notched at the tip. The tiny cream-coloured fragrant flowers are borne in rounded clusters. Occurring in mountain forest and coastal scrub from the southwestern Cape through to Natal, it blooms from winter to late spring, and produces its striking 3-horned orange-yellow fruits from winter to the end of summer.

There are 5 species in tropical and southern Africa, but only 1 other occurs in this area. *P. rostratus* of ravine forests has a pointed leaf up to 90 mm by 50 mm and produces orange fruits with many horns.

RHAMNACEAE

Phylica ericoides
A much-branched, rather stiff neatly-rounded shrub to 900 mm with crowded heath-like leaves 5-8 mm long. The minute flowers are densely crowded above an involucre of small brown scale-like bracts, to form a posy head 4-7 mm across. The heads are often massed towards the tips of the branches, especially in the coarser form found near the sea. Widespread on dunes and lower coastal mountain slopes from Paarl and the Cape Peninsula to Port Elizabeth and south tropical Africa, it may bloom at any time of the year.

There are about 150 species in Africa and the offshore islands, of which some 23 are found in this area.

Rhus laevigata   *Laurophyllus capensis*

Pterocelastrus tricuspidatus   *Phylica ericoides*

RHAMNACEAE

Phylica spicata
A much-branched sturdy shrub to 2 m with velvety branches. The sharp pointed leaves are up to 25 mm by 12 mm, shiny above and pale-felted below, with the edges tightly rolled under near the tip but progressively unfurled towards the base. The crowded flowers, attracting hosts of bees when open, are borne in woolly spikes which may vary in shape, being only slightly elongated or up to 75 mm long. The spikes are borne singly or in groups at the tips of the branches. It occurs on mountain slopes from Clanwilliam to Worcester, Tulbagh to Stellenbosch and Piketberg. The plant illustrated is a young one found at Jonkershoek. (Apr-Aug)

Phylica lasiocarpa
A low, spreading, many-stemmed, rather loose shrub to 600 mm resprouting from a fire-resistant stump. The rough upcurved leaves, 6-12 mm long, may be heathlike with edges tightly rolled underneath, or openbacked, almost flat and 3 mm wide. The flowers may be grouped into small rather loose heads 5-6 mm across, as in this illustration, or the heads may be posy-like. It is very common on the lower, drier slopes from Stellenbosch to Hermanus and Bredasdorp. (Dec-Apr)

Phylica gracilis
A slender, hairy, much-branched shrub to 1 m or more with leaves to 10 mm long. The leaf edges roll under to varying degrees, partly concealing the woolly reverse. The white woolly flowers are borne in clusters at the tips of short branchlets at the ends of the main stems and the fruit is a top-shaped purple-brown capsule. Occurring on sandy slopes and flats from Malmesbury and Stellenbosch to Bredasdorp, it blooms mainly from December to April although plants at Hermanus, where this specimen was photographed, flower from June to September. (Dec-Sept)

Phylica pubescens   Featherhead   Veerkoppie
A dense erect, moderately-branched shrub to 2 m with shaggy, silky branches and younger leaves. The rather crowded mature leaves are 25-35 mm long, spreading outwards and upwards. They may be open-backed with a pale felt-like undersurface, or tightly rolled underneath. The single heads resemble plumes and are up to 50 mm across. Quite common on dry lower mountain slopes and flats in inland areas from Worcester to Stellenbosch and Cape Peninsula to Riversdale. (May-Aug)

The similar golden-headed *P. plumosa* with almost hairless branches and outcurving, rather shorter leaves, also occurs in this area.

Phylica spicata *Phylica lasiocarpa*

Phylica gracilis *Phylica pubescens*

MALVACEAE

Anisodontea scabrosa
An erect, harsh-textured, hairy, often sticky and aromatic shrub 2-3 m tall with leaves variable in shape, the lower 20-70 mm long but much reduced in size among the flowers. The hibiscus-like red to pinkish to off-white flowers occur singly or in small groups in the axils of the leaves, have the stamens gathered into a central column, and produce a 9-15 chambered fruit. Widely distributed in diverse soils, often in disturbed ground from Saldanha Bay to the eastern Cape, mostly on the coastal plain, it blooms all the year round.

There are 20 species from the southwestern Cape to Lesotho and Namibia, but only 1 occurs in this area.

Hibiscus trionum
A coarse, often straggly, harsh bristly annual up to 250 mm or more. The leaves are lobed or deeply cut, and the yellow flowers with black centres are 25-40 mm across. The calyx becomes inflated as the fruit ripens. It occurs as a widespread and common weed of cultivation in the warmer parts of the Old World, often in damp places. (Sept-Feb)

There are about 300 species worldwide of which 50 occur in South Africa and possibly 5 in this area. Two more have similar flowers: *H. aethiopicus* is a dwarf perennial with oval serrated leaves; *H. diversifolius* has prickly stems.

STERCULIACEAE

Hermannia sp.
A low shrublet with numerous short bare rough stems to 250 mm from a persistent rootstock. It has a dense canopy of oval glossy green leaves with veins hairy on the reverse and a toothed edge. The very abundant flowers, borne in drooping heads, are about 8 mm long, with a pale shortly hairy calyx. It is found particularly in disturbed areas on the coastal plain, and is either an undescribed species or a hybrid. (Sept-Oct)

Hermannia rudis   Doll's roses   Poprosies
A low, straggly shrublet, resprouting and flowering profusely after fire, with branchlets and leaves covered with rough hairs. The leaves are wedge-shaped with a coarse-toothed tip. The flowers may be pink or pale yellow to orange, and are borne singly or in pairs near the tips of the branchlets. The petals are twisted and protrude to a greater or lesser extent from the bristly calyx, which is often red in colour. Occurring in dry sandy or rocky places on slopes facing the sea from the Cape Peninsula to Swellendam. (May-Oct)

There are about 300 species in the dry tropics and subtropics of Africa, Australia and America, of which perhaps 8 occur in this area.

Anisodontea scabrosa

Hibiscus trionum

Hermannia sp.

Hermannia rudis

STERCULIACEAE

Hermannia ternifolia
A sprawling shrub with trailing or erect branchlets which often root where buried. The grey-velvety stalked leaves are broadest towards the scalloped tip. The flowers have a strong sweet scent and may be orange-yellow, red or marmalade colour and have a puffed up calyx. They are usually borne singly on short stout stalks in the axils of the leaves. Occurring on sand dunes or coastal limestone from Malmesbury and the Cape Peninsula to Bredasdorp. (July-Oct)

VIOLACEAE

Viola decumbens
A weak, sprawling perennial to 300 mm with narrow leaves and blue-mauve or white flowers, sometimes yellow in the throat, typically violet-shaped and sometimes scented. Quite common on lower slopes in rocky, sandy or stony places from Ceres and Worcester to Montagu and throughout this area. (July-Dec)

There are about 500 species worldwide of which 2 occur in South Africa and only 1 in this area.

FRANKENIACEAE

Frankenia pulverulenta — Sea-heath
A small, prostrate perennial, with simple, usually open-backed, narrow leaves which are often reddish and single lilac 5 mm long flowers. It is found on the seashore or in salt pans from the Orange River mouth to Port Elizabeth. (Sept-Jan)

There are about 80 species worldwide, all tending to be associated with salty soils; 3 occur in South Africa and 1 other in this area. *F. repens* has the edges of its leaves tightly rolled under, and 10 mm long pink flowers in groups.

PENAEACEAE

Penaea cneorum
A tall lanky shrub to 2 m or more. The oval sessile leaves with straight points on the tips, are arranged in opposite pairs, giving a 4-sided look to the stems, as is the case with all members of this family. The flowers, up to 10 mm long, have no petals and are borne in clusters at the branch tips. They are greenish-yellow, becoming brick red with age. It occurs in moist, often steep places from the Hottentots Holland mountains to Port Elizabeth and blooms throughout the year.

There are 3 species confined to the fynbos area of the Cape, of which 1 other occurs in this area: the common *P. mucronata* of lower open mountain slopes and flats is a much shorter, rounded plant with yellow flowers and somewhat incurved leaftip points.

Hermannia ternifolia

Viola decumbens

Frankenia pulverulenta

Penaea cneorum

PENAEACEAE

Saltera sarcocolla   Vlieëbos
A rather untidy, sparsely-branched shrub to 1 m with leathery, rounded, overlapping leaves and terminal flowerheads of 1-6 flowers surrounded by sticky bract-like leaves. The flowers are pink, often with white markings, but a less common white single-flowered form occurs in the Hangklip area. It is common on flats and slopes from the Cape Peninsula, inland to Franschhoek, along the coast to Bredasdorp and blooms throughout the year.

There is only 1 species.

Sonderothamnus speciosus
A sparsely branched erect shrub to 600 mm with broad overlapping 6-10 mm long leaves neatly arranged on the upper stems, each with a round wart at the tip. On older plants the lower stems are naked. The crowded pink flowers are surrounded by fringed bracts. Occasional on sandy mountain slopes in the Klein River mountains. (July-Oct)

There are 2 species, both found in this area. The smaller, *S. petraeus*, occurs in crevices in vertical sandstone cliffs from Cape Hangklip to Kleinmond.

THYMELAEACEAE

A family recognizable by having bark which tears into long strips. The flowers always have a well-developed calyx with 4-5 lobes, often resembling petals, and petals absent or reduced to scale-like or fleshy lobes at the mouth of the calyx.

Lachnaea densiflora
A much-branched shrublet to 300 mm with narrow pointed leaves up to 10 mm long. The pink or cream flowers, each less than 5 mm long, have a woolly calyx, no petals, and are borne in well-defined round heads. Occurring on sandy flats or lower slopes, which may be seasonally damp, from the Cape Peninsula to Bredasdorp. (Sept-Jan)

There are about 29 species in the southwestern Cape, of which 6 occur in this area.

Struthiola tomentosa   Roemenaggie
A slender silvery-haired shrublet to 450 mm with closely overlapping oval leaves. The sweetly-scented yellow flowers, tinged with orange-red, are hairy on the outside with 12 fingerlike petals radiating from stiff golden hairs. The sessile flowers occur singly or occasionally in pairs in the axils of the leaves. It occurs on mountain slopes from Caledon to Swellendam and blooms all year.

There are about 40 species in Africa south of the equator of which 10 occur in this area. Two other species have 12 petals: *S. martiana*, with white or pink flowers, and the resprouting *S. mundii* with hairless yellow flowers.

Saltera sarcocolla

Sonderothamnus speciosus

Lachnaea densiflora

Struthiola tomentosa

THYMELAEACEAE

Gnidia juniperifolia
A hairless, sprawling or erect, resprouting shrub to 500 mm with 10-12 mm long narrow oval leaves with pointed tips. The 6-8 mm long yellow flowers, borne singly or in pairs at the tips of the branches, have a long tubular calyx and 4 membranous petals visible in the mouth. It is common on mountain slopes from Paarl and the Cape Peninsula to Riversdale, and can be found in bloom at any time of the year.

There are some 150 species found mostly in Africa with 47 in the southern Cape of which 15 or more may be found in this area.

Gnidia oppositifolia
An erect slender shrub up to 3 m tall with overlapping pairs of smooth oval, pointed leaves about 10 mm long. The pale yellow hairy flowers, with a 16 mm long tube, have 4 fingerlike petals in the mouth, and are borne in groups raised above the topmost leaves. Occurring in wet places and on stream-banks on mountain slopes from Clanwilliam to the eastern Cape and Transvaal, it may bloom at any time of the year.

G. tomentosa has 4 yellow fingerlike petals but silky, alternate leaves.

Struthiola myrsinites
An open willowy shrub to 2 m tall, often producing dense clusters of branches towards the top of the main stems. The stems are clothed quite closely with pairs of narrow, hairless, pointed leaves up to 12 mm long and 5 mm wide. The flowers, about 22 mm long, are pale to bright pink in bud, but open up white or pale pink. They are hairless on the outside and have 8 fingerlike petals projecting from a halo of pale bristles at the mouth of the flower. Occurring widely in sandy soil, often near watercourses from the Gifberg to the eastern Cape, it can be found in bloom at any time of the year.

Other species with 8 petals are *S. eckloniana*, which has leaves only 2 mm wide and occurs on rocky slopes; the hairy-flowered *S. confusa*, richly perfumed at dusk; and *S. salteri* with leaves in 3's or 4's.

Gnidia pinifolia
An erect single-stemmed shrub to 1 m tall with narrow, almost needlelike crowded leaves up to 16 mm long. The hairy flowers, borne in groups at the branch tips, are sometimes pinkish in the bud, but open white. The tube is 12 mm long and there are 4 fingerlike petals. Occurring on flats and low to middle slopes from Piketberg to the eastern Cape and Transvaal, it can bloom at any time of the year.

Gnidia juniperifolia

Gnidia oppositifolia

Struthiola myrsinites

Gnidia pinifolia

THYMELAEACEAE

Struthiola striata   Katstertjie Roemenaggie Veertjie
A shrub to 1 m tall, hairy when young but becoming hairless, with pairs of oval 10 mm by 3 mm, overlapping, ribbed leaves. The 10 mm long creamy flowers are clothed with hairs outside and have 4 fingerlike petals surrounded by pale bristles. Occurring on coastal flats and lower slopes from the Cape Peninsula to Mossel Bay and on to the eastern Cape. (Sept-June)

In this area only 1 other, the reddish-flowered *S. tetralepis* of upper mountain slopes, has 4 petals.

Gnidia squarrosa
A variable, branched, rather rigid shrub to 1,3 m tall, with narrow lance-shaped leaves 8 mm by 1 mm. The creamy-green to yellow flowers are pink-flushed with a 7 mm long tube and 8 fingerlike petals in the mouth. Occurring on limestone or sandy slopes near the coast from the Cape Peninsula to the eastern Cape and Natal. (June-Oct)

Other creamy-yellow species which may be found near the coast include *G. chrysophylla,* with densely hairy silvery leaves in pairs and 4 petals; 2 others without petals, the shrubby yellow to brown flowered *G. laxa* and the slender cream-flowered *G. spicata.*

APIACEAE

Heteroptilis suffruticosa   Sea parsley
A hairless, branched, prostrate or erect perennial up to 500 mm tall, with fleshy, divided, parsley-like leaves up to 80 mm long, with a stalk half the length. The flowers are in clusters up to 30 mm across, enlarging to double this width when in fruit. Occurring on dunes, flats and sandy slopes from the Cape to Natal. (Dec-Apr)

There is only 1 species.

Peucedanum galbanum   Blister bush Bergseldery
A resinous-scented, sturdy, branching shrub to 3 m tall, with stalked compound leaves attached all along the stems and bearing diamond-shaped leaflets. The insignificant flowers are borne in a compound umbel. Occurring on mid to upper slopes, often in moist or sheltered places, from Piketberg to Riversdale. (July-Feb)
BEWARE OF THIS PLANT. It is known to provoke in some people, and in some conditions, quite savage skin irritation, characteristically delayed for a day or two. The worst reactions seem to arise when one is perspiring, and when the plant is bruised.

There are about 170 species in Africa and Eurasia, of which 9 may occur in this area, but none resemble this species.

Struthiola striata *Gnidia squarrosa*

Heteroptilis suffruticosa *Peucedanum galbanum*

APIACEAE

Centella triloba
A sturdy sprawling hairless perennial usually hanging from rocks, with woody older stems and ribbed branches up to 0,5 m long. It bears tufts of wedge-shaped leaves, 20-50 mm long, toothed at the apex and narrowing gradually below into leafstalks up to 60 mm long. It occurs on mountains from the Cape Peninsula to Caledon and Robertson, and is more abundant at higher altitudes. (July-Apr)

There are about 40 species in the southern hemisphere of which some 17 occur in this area, but there is only 1 other with a similar leaf; the hairy, stout and erect *C. difformis*.

Hermas quinquedentata
A perennial to 300 mm with a tuft of stiff, glossy, bright green leaves borne near the ground, hairless above and white-woolly below. A creamy-yellow head of flowers about 20 mm across is borne on a typically unbranched stalk with scattered bracts. Occurring in rock crevices at middle altitudes throughout most of this area. (Jan-Apr)

There are 9 species confined to the Cape, of which 4 others are found in this area. Two species are of similar proportions but have branched flower-stalks; *H. quercifolia* of damp places with rosettes of flannelly oak-like leaves; and *H. ciliata*, with eyelash-fringed, oval, long-stalked leaves.

Hermas villosa   Tontelblaar
A robust shrub to 1 m, with a group of very shiny, rigid, carrot-scented leaves at ground level. They have a densely white-haired reverse, and are up to 150 mm long and 60 mm wide. The long, smooth, naked flowering stem bears globose flower clusters about 40 mm across. Extremely common on dry mountain slopes from the Cape Peninsula to Caledon. (Dec-May)

The resinous *H. gigantea*, of the inland mountains, has altogether woolly leaves double this size, and deep purple flowers.

Lichtensteinia lacera   Kalmus Kalmoes
An edible-rooted perennial with large leaves, resembling a spiky form of rhubarb. The rigid branched flowering stems grow to 1,25 m (the illustrated one is unusually short), and emerge from a tuft of black fibres. The yellowish flower clusters are flat-topped. Occurring on the flats and lower slopes at Jonkershoek, and the Cape Peninsula. (Jan-Mar)

There are 7 species in South Africa, of which this is the only one in this area.

Centella triloba

Hermas quinquedentata

Hermas villosa

Lichtensteinia lacera

APIACEAE

Arctopus echinatus   Platdoring   Pokkiesdoring
A prickly perennial with underground stems, and a rosette of hair-fringed spiny leaves 40-100 mm long and wide, pressed to the ground. The male flowers are pink or white, and the female yellow-green, borne on separate plants, and they are surrounded by 3-spined leafy bracts. Common on flats and lower slopes from Namaqualand to Uitenhage. (May-Aug)

There are about 4 species confined to the fynbos areas of the Cape of which 1 other occurs in this area, the rarer *A. monacanthus* with single-spined leafy bracts.

ERICACEAE

Erica, a vast genus which has some 663 species in Africa and Eurasia, of which 636 occur in southern Africa and over 200 in this area. *Erica* flowers have 4 joined petals and 8 stamens. The edges of the leaves are usually rolled under.

Erica cerinthoides   Fire heath   Rooihartjie
An erect or sprawling shrub, occasionally to 1,8 m when protected from fire, but now rarely seen so tall. It has relatively few branches arising from a woody fire-resistant stump known as a lignotuber. The leaves are 6-16 mm long. The 22-34 mm long, hairy, crimson or rarely pink or white flowers are borne in terminal clusters. The stamens and stigma are concealed within the tube. Occurring on sandy flats and slopes from Vanrhynsdorp along most of the escarpment mountains to Natal and the Zoutpansberg. Being one of the first plants to flower after a veld fire, it blooms at any season of the year.

Erica cumuliflora
An erect branching shrub to 450 mm tall with fairly well-spaced leaves 4-6 mm long. The dry-textured clusters of 5-12 flowers are borne in drooping densely-packed heads at the tips of the branches. What appear in the illustration to be dark brown stamens projecting from the mouth of the flower are in fact the lobes of the petals. The stamens are concealed within. It occurs on dry middle slopes and upper peaty plateaux, often in dense stands, on the coastal mountains of the Caledon district through to Bredasdorp. (Sept-Nov)

Erica lanuginosa
An erect woody shrublet to 600 mm with needlelike leaves about 20 mm long. The flowers are usually in 3's at the ends of the branches, but sometimes singly or in pairs. They are covered with very short velvety hairs, but appear smooth and are hard in texture. The petals are split almost to the base and have erect lobes which meet in a point. The stamens and stigma are concealed. It occurs in scattered colonies amongst rocks in the Klein River mountains at mid to high altitude. (July-Oct)

Arctopus echinatus

Erica cerinthoides

Erica cumuliflora

Erica lanuginosa

ERICACEAE

Erica holosericea
An erect shrub to 900 mm, but usually much smaller, with few branches and narrow, sharp-tipped leaves 10-16 mm long. The soft, velvety flowers are 7-10 mm long, mostly in groups of 3 on very short side branchlets. As the petals fade the lobes darken and close to a point, whilst the sepals remain colourful for quite a while. It is found on moist south-facing mountain slopes from the Kogelberg to Bredasdorp. (Sept-Nov)

Erica perspicua   Prince of Wales heath
An erect shrub 1 m or more high with willowy branches and tufts of very short usually hairy leaves. The softly-hairy tubular flowers, 16-25 mm long, grow singly on short side-branches, forming a loose spike-like head. The colour varies from pure white, through rose to almost purple, usually with paler lobes, the colour being most intense at high altitudes. It occurs in damp places from sea level to upper mountain slopes in the Caledon district. (Sept-Apr)

Erica imbricata
An erect twiggy shrub to 800 mm with crowded leaves, 3-5 mm long, often tufted on very short side branchlets. The flowers, which are sometimes slightly sticky, are in groups of 3 or more at the tips of the branchlets, and have prominent sepals which almost cover the petals. The dark stamens project beyond the petals. It is usually white but pale pink to reddish forms are also found. It is extremely common on sandy flats and mountain slopes throughout this area. (Feb-Nov)

Erica fastigiata   Four sisters heath
An erect or spreading shrub to 500 mm with crowded hairless leaves. The flowers are borne at the branch tips in upright groups of 4, each with a narrow tube and 4 spreading lobes. In the typical form the lobes are somewhat rounded and have a darker central 'eye'. It is found mostly in damp places on flats and mountain slopes from Bain's Kloof to Caledon. (Aug-Jan)

In the Hermanus mountains a variety, *E. fastigiata* var. *coventryana*, may be found with more sharply pointed petal lobes and without a dark 'eye'; another *E. fastigata* var. *immaculata,* with slightly sticky flowers, occurs at Franschhoek and blooms in December.

Erica holosericea

Erica perspicua

Erica imbricata

Erica fastigiata

ERICACEAE

Erica nana
A sturdy sprawling shrub with stiff twisted branches and short hairless leaves. The flowers are hard in texture and have an almost waxy sheen. They are borne in 4's at the tips of the branchlets in such profusion that the whole plant may become a sheet of yellow. It is usually found hanging from cliff faces or sprawling over rocks from Kogelberg to the Hottentots Holland mountains. (Sept-Oct)

The flowers are almost identical to those of *E. foliacea* but the latter is a stout erect shrub to 1 m.

Erica grandiflora var. exsurgens
A robust erect shrub to 1,5 m with hairless incurved leaves up to 20 mm long. The curved tubular flowers are borne singly in an untidy spike in the axils of the leaves. They are hairless, sometimes sticky, and up to 28 mm long. The usual colour is orange-red, but the variety in this illustration which grows at Jonkershoek, is yellow. The stamens and stigma project beyond the mouth of the flower. It occurs on the inland mountain slopes in the north of this area, and from Tulbagh to Riversdale. (June-Aug)

Erica tenax
An erect slender plant to 1 m becoming more shrubby with age or when growing in an exposed position. It has crowded leaves up to 10 mm long, and very sticky flowers 27 mm long, arising singly in the leaf axils on 15 mm stalks. The stamens are visible at the mouth of the flower, with the style protruding beyond them. It has a very limited distribution in sheltered valleys in the mountains behind Kleinmond, but occurs there in profusion. (Nov-Mar)

The equally sticky, closely related *E. thomae,* with white or occasionally purple flowers, occurs in the same area.

Erica patersonia   Mealie heath
An erect plant to 1 m with few branches and crowded overlapping leaves 8-12 mm long. The dry-textured flowers form a dense spike towards the ends of the branches. It is found on marshy flats near the sea at Betty's Bay and Kleinmond. (Apr-Aug)

It is also still to be seen at Cape Point, but has been exterminated at Hermanus due to overpicking and housing development.

Erica nana

Erica grandiflora var. *exsurgens*

Erica tenax

Erica patersonia

ERICACEAE

Erica irbyana
An erect shrub to 450 mm with wiry stems and narrow leaves 4-8 mm long. The sticky bottle-shaped flowers are on stalks up to 14 mm long, in groups of from 3 to 8 at the ends of the branches. The deep red sepals contrast with the glistening pink petals. It occurs on lower slopes from Hawston to Bredasdorp. (Oct-Jan)

Erica retorta   Bottle heath
Closely related to the previous species, and to *E. aristata* below, this plant is quite distinct. It grows to about 450 mm in height with somewhat straggly branches. The tiny leaves are thick and rigid and curve up at the tips, ending in a long bristle. The flowers are variable in length, from 8-25 mm, and occur in heads of up to 8 or more flowers on long stalks. They are extremely sticky, clear pink, usually with darker pink lobes. It is common on dry mountain slopes at Betty's Bay and Kleinmond. (Oct-Apr)

Erica massonii   Masson's heath
An erect shrub to about 1 m with spreading branches, becoming leggy with age. The closely overlapping leaves are 6-10 mm long and are fringed with long hairs. Extremely sticky red or orange flowers with green tips, with up to 22 flowers per head, make this an unmistakeable species. It occurs on sandy or rocky slopes up to 1 000 m, from Hottentots Holland to Hangklip and the Klein River mountains. (Oct-May)

Erica aristata
An erect woody shrub to 600 mm with stiff down-curved sharply-pointed leaves 5-6 mm long. The long tubular flowers with their short frilly lobes are very sticky and occur in groups of 4 at the ends of the branches. Found only in a small area on the mountains between Hawston and Stanford, but quite common there. (Aug-Oct)

Erica irbyana *Erica retorta*

Erica massonii *Erica aristata*

ERICACEAE

Erica sphaeroidea
An erect shrub to 500 mm with open light brown branches. Stems and leaves are covered with bristly gland-tipped hairs giving them a soft slightly clammy feel. The leaves are spreading, usually oval and open-backed, and up to 10 mm long. The oval pink or white flowers are somewhat sticky and usually covered with fine velvety hairs. They occur in groups of 3 at the branch-tips or scattered in the leaf axils. The stamens and style project slightly beyond the petals. Frequent on lower and middle mountain slopes from Du Toit's Kloof to Jonkershoek and the Hottentots Holland mountains, it may be in flower at any time of the year. *E. racemosa*, which grows in the same areas, is similar but has much smaller needlelike leaves and all the flowers are borne in the leaf axils.

Erica longiaristata
A slender shrub to 600 mm which has narrow overlapping 2-4 mm long leaves. The tiny urn-shaped flowers are about 5 mm long, have spreading lobes, and are smooth and firm-textured. They grow singly or in small groups in the leaf axils and form dense clusters at the ends of the branches. The stigma and stamens are not visible. It usually grows in large open colonies on sandy flats and lower mountain slopes, from Hangklip to Bredasdorp. (Dec-Apr)

The very similar *E. pulchella* occurs in the same areas and differs only in having erect petal lobes and a more closed mouth.

Erica sessiliflora
An erect robust shrub to 2 m in height with narrow leaves only 2-4 mm long. The pale green tubular flowers grow in spikes near the tops of the branches. It can always be recognised even when not in flower, by the unique fleshy sepals which turn red and increase in size around the fruits and remain on the plant for several years. It is widespread in damp localities on coastal mountains and further inland from Piketberg to Humansdorp. (Apr-Sept)

Erica subdivaricata
A variable shrub, sometimes quite sturdy to 1 m tall, but more often low and spreading, with short narrow crowded leaves. The creamy-white flowers grow in groups of 4 at the branch-tips. Common on sandy flats from the Cape Peninsula to Port Elizabeth. (Jan-July)

Erica sphaeroidea

Erica longiaristata

Erica sessiliflora

Erica subdivaricata

ERICACEAE

Erica cruenta Crimson heath
An erect shrub to 1 m tall with narrow overlapping leaves 5-8 mm long. The smooth, shiny, dark red flowers, borne singly at the tips of short branchlets, are up to 25 mm long. The stigmas are sometimes just visible at the mouth, with the style projecting slightly. It occurs on lower clay slopes from the Hottentots Holland to Riversdale and regenerates rapidly from a fire-resistant stump after veld fires. It is now rare due to agricultural expansion. (Feb-Nov)

Erica longifolia
An erect shrub to 900 mm with open branches bearing crowded overlapping leaves up to 20 mm long. The flowers may be green, white, red, or pink and even bi-coloured. They usually have short hairs and are somewhat sticky, and form a short whorl or spike near the tips of the branches. Common and widespread on mountain slopes from Paarl and Worcester to Bredasdorp, its flowering time depends on the locality.

This species is replaced by the very similar *E. onosmiflora* in the Hermanus mountains. There is very little to distinguish the 2 species but the yellow-green flowers of the latter have a rough, hairy texture.

Erica plukenetii Hangertjie
An extremely variable, erect shrub with stiff branches and incurving, crowded leaves up to 20 mm long. The flowers may be white, greenish, pink, red-orange or reddish-purple, and have a tubular corolla up to 18 mm long. The anthers project in a tight cone which opens explosively when levered apart, propelling the pollen onto the head of a foraging bird pollinator. Occurring on flats and mountains from Namaqualand to Mossel Bay, it is one of the most widespread and common members of the fynbos flora. It may bloom at any time of the year.

It is often confused with *E. coccinea*, equally common on dry lower slopes, but the latter species has short leaves arranged in tufts up the branches.

Erica mammosa
An erect slender-branched shrub to about 1,2 m with narrow overlapping leaves 6-10 mm long. The drooping short-stalked flowers emerge from the axils of the leaves and form a loose spike. Like the previous 2 species, this is another that is very variably coloured, being found in white, orange, pink, purple and green as well as the commoner red form shown here. They are distinguished from all other species of similar habit by having 4 dents at the base of the corolla tube. Widespread throughout the southern Cape from Clanwilliam to Caledon. (Dec-Apr)

Erica cruenta *Erica longifolia*

Erica plukenetii *Erica mammosa*

PLUMBAGINACEAE

Limonium scabrum   Sea lavender   Brakblommetjie
A much-branched shrublet to 250 mm with sandpapery stems and bluegreen leaves up to 80 mm by 10 mm in a tuft at ground level. The flowers are 9-12 mm long. Occurring from the Cape Peninsula to the Fish River near the sea, and often temporarily submerged in estuaries and vleis. (Oct-May)

There are about 100 species in the northern hemisphere, Africa and Australia in coastal and arid regions, of which 17 occur in southern Africa and 4 in this area. Two have similar leaves; the mauve *L. depauperatum* with additional small leaf tufts on the flowering stems and the white flowered *L. anthericoides; L. kraussianum* has needle-like basal leaves.

OLEACEAE

Olea exasperata   Bastard olive   Basterolienhout
A shrub or small tree to 8 m but normally less, with rough branchlets bearing pairs of narrow, leathery, oblong leaves 40-85 mm by 6-15 mm, dull green below. Clusters of white flowers 1-6 mm across are borne at the tips of leafless, angularly-branched twigs, followed by purplish-black fleshy oval fruits. Occurring mainly in dune scrub on the coastal belt from the Cape Peninsula eastward to East London. (June-Feb)

There are about 50 species from Africa, the Mediterranean and Asia, of which 4 occur in South Africa, with a further 2 in this area.

GENTIANACEAE

Villarsia capensis
A soft perennial with groups of long-stalked, oval leaves and 12 mm long fringed flowers borne on branched stems. Occurring in wet places or in open water from the Cape Peninsula and Worcester to Humansdorp. When growing in water the leaf and flowering stems elongate so that they reach the surface. (Oct-Feb)

There are about 10 species mainly in Australia, with only this representative in South Africa.

Orphium frutescens
A spectacular, erect shrub to 800 mm with soft, usually hairy, rather thick leaves about 50 mm long. The stalked pink, occasionally white flowers, up to 30 mm long, contain anthers twisted like barley-sugar. Occurring commonly near the shore on sandy, often marshy brackish flats from Clanwilliam to George. (Nov-Feb)

There is only 1 species.

Limonium scabrum

Olea exasperata

Villarsia capensis

Orphium frutescens

GENTIANACEAE

Chironia decumbens
A sparsely-branched perennial, with some creeping stems rooting at intervals, others erect to 300 mm, and pairs of narrowly elliptic soft leaves up to 43 mm by 8 mm. The stalked flowers, about 25 mm long, have calyx lobes split almost to the base, and petals with a strong ridge up the back. Occurring in marshy coastal sites or at the edge of lakes and vleis from the Cape Peninsula to the eastern Cape. (Oct-Jan)

There are about 30 species in Africa and Madagascar of which 7 occur in this area. The shade-loving *C. melampyrifolia* is another straggler, distinguished by being sticky and having heart-shaped leaves.

Chironia jasminoides
An erect non-sticky perennial to 900 mm with sparsely-branched 4-angled stems, with narrow ridges at the angles bearing pairs of narrow oval or oblong leaves 20-70 mm long. The flowers, 24-38 mm long are borne on a flowerstalk 10-100 mm long. Occurring on mountain slopes in sand or on shale, or in damp coastal areas from Paarl to Riversdale. (Aug-Jan)

C. stokoei is the only other non-sticky, upright species in this area, and is distinguished by a pair of sepal-like bracts attached to the flowerstalk immediately below the flower.

Chironia linoides ssp. nana
A low shrublet to 200 mm, with several slender branches from near the base of the stem, and narrow widely-spaced leaves up to 25 mm long. The calyx is split to below the middle and at least 1 of the lobes stands away from the corolla tube. The flowers are 12-15 mm long and are borne singly or in 2's or 3's at the branch tips. It grows on sandy flats and mountain slopes from Worcester to Bredasdorp. (Oct-Jan)

The only other low-growing non-sticky species in this area is the dense shrublet, *C. baccifera* which favours sand dunes, with similar flowers followed by bright orange-red berries.

Chironia tetragona
An erect, rather rigid annual or biennial with few branches and 4-angled winged stems. The leaves are of variable width from 1-10 mm and up to 30 mm long, and are thick, rigid, slightly wrinkled and often sticky. The flowers, about 30 mm long, are also sticky and are thickened in the throat where the stamens are attached. Occurring in a variety of habitats on the coastal plain from the Cape Peninsula to the eastern Cape. (Oct-Jan)

Chironia decumbens

Chironia jasminoides

Chironia linoides ssp. *nana*

Chironia tetragona

ASCLEPIADACEAE

Asclepias cancellata — Wild cotton   Gansies   Katoenbos
A rigid velvety shrub to 1 m with milky sap, bearing leathery, paired leaves up to 50 mm by 32 mm, with a whitish reverse. Clusters of cream, brown and maroon flowers are borne on sturdy stalks in the axils of the leaves. They are followed by oval pods 50 mm long or more, covered with fingerlike projections and enclosing seeds which have silky parachutes to aid their dispersal. Occurring from Namaqualand to the eastern Cape and Karoo, usually as isolated plants, it blooms most of the year.

There are about 150 species in Africa, Arabia and America, with only 1 other in this area: *A. fruticosa*, with leaves several times longer than broad.

BORAGINACEAE

Echiostachys ecklonianus
A perennial with woody underground stems producing tufts of leaves and flowering shoots each year, which are seldom more than 360 mm high. The lowest leaves are up to 120 mm by 18 mm but are much smaller on the flowering shoot. The flowerhead can be up to 80 mm long, purplish or reddish and strongly scented. It grows in sandy or gravelly soil on the lower mountain slopes throughout this area and at Bredasdorp. (Aug-Dec)

There are 3 species in the fynbos, with 1 other in this area: *E. incanus* has white or cream faintly-scented flowers.

Lobostemon fruticosus — Agtdaegeneesbos   Luibos
A rounded shrub to 1 m with densely hairy branches, and hairy leaves 15-60 mm by 5-12 mm. The funnel-shaped flowers are shortly hairy, up to 25 mm long and in subtle shades of pink and blue, varying on the same plant. Occasionally a white form is found. It grows in sandy places from Namaqualand to Uniondale. (Aug-Oct)

There are 28 species in South Africa, mostly in the fynbos, of which 5 occur in this area.

STILBACEAE

Stilbe ericoides
An erect, neatly rounded or straggling shrublet to 800 mm, branching chiefly at the base. It has hard, heath-like leaves 3-6 mm long, and pink or mauve flowers in a dense spike at the top of each stem. Each flower has 4 projecting stamens and a circle of white hairs in the throat. Occurring on sandy flats and limestone hills from Malmesbury and the Cape Peninsula to Uitenhage. (Apr-Sept)

There are 6 species confined to the Cape, 5 of which are found in this area.

Asclepias cancellata

Echiostachys ecklonianus

Lobostemon fruticosus

Stilbe ericoides

STILBACEAE

Stilbe mucronata
A sturdy contorted shrub to 1 m with 4-8 mm long crowded leaves bending backwards when mature. The grey-mauve flowers with 4 stamens and white hairs in the throat are crowded into dense, rounded, white-woolly heads about 12 mm across. Occasional at mid to high altitudes in rock crevices and among rocks from this area to Swellendam. (May-Oct)

LAMIACEAE

Salvia chamelaeagnea Bloublommetjiesalie Afrikaanse salie
A much-branched rough-textured shrub to 2 m with faintly 4-sided stems. It has pairs of simple, leathery, oval, almost hairless leaves with smooth or slightly toothed edges. Distinctly 2-lipped blueish flowers with or without white markings are borne at the ends of leafless branchlets. Widespread on slopes and flats from Namaqualand to the Oudtshoorn area. (Nov-May)

There are about 900 species worldwide with about 40 in South Africa and 2 others in this area. The rather similar blue flowered *S. africana-caerulea* has a calyx which enlarges around the fruit.

Stachys aethiopica Katbossie
A straggling perennial with bristly 4-sided stems up to 500 mm long and pairs of triangular leaves up to 24 mm long with scalloped edges. The pink or white flowers have a 2-lipped corolla with a tube less than 12 mm long and 4 projecting stamens. Occurring most often in shade in fynbos or forest from the Cedarberg to the eastern Cape and on to tropical Africa. (Aug-Sept)

There are about 450 species worldwide in temperate regions, of which 2 have been recorded in this area.

Salvia africana-lutea Wild sage Strandsalie
A dense shrub to 2 m with aromatic grey leaves and 2-lipped flowers of an unusual rich tan colour. The anthers are concealed beneath the upper lip and swivel downwards when a visiting animal attempts to gain access to the copious nectar. The calyx remains on the plant, increasing slightly in size, after the flowers have faded. This once common and widespread plant, now becoming scarce because of the development of its habitat by man, provides an essential food supply for sunbirds when the proteas on the mountains are out of flower. It occurs in the coastal dune vegetation, and also further inland in dry fynbos, from the Gifberg to Port Elizabeth. (June-Dec)

Stilbe mucronata

Stachys aethiopica

Salvia chamelaeagnea

Salvia africana-lutea

SOLANACEAE

Solanum guineense
An erect non-spiny shrub to 2 m with smooth oval leaves up to 50 mm by 28 mm. The fruit is a berry some 25 mm across. Occurring in forest margins, lower slopes and coastal dunes from Piketberg to the eastern Cape. (Nov-June)

This is a cosmopolitan genus of over 2 000 species, many of them poisonous, containing such important plants as the potato, the tomato and tobacco. There are about 30 species in South Africa, including some introduced weeds, with about 7 in this area. Another spineless species found on the coast is the sprawling *S. quadrangulare* with purple terminal flowers.

RETZIACEAE

Retzia capensis　　　　　　　　　　　　　　　　　　　　Heuningblom
A stiffly erect many-stemmed shrub up to 2 m, but usually less, with a fire-resistant stump. Its narrow leaves may be dark green or rust-coloured, with tightly rolled edges. The flowers are about 25 mm long. It is found on low to middle slopes of the coastal mountains from the Hottentots Holland to Bredasdorp and the Riviersonderend range. (Sept-Mar)

It is the only member of the family.

SCROPHULARIACEAE

Halleria elliptica　　　　　　　　　　　　Bush honeysuckle　Notsung
An erect shrub to 2 m with pairs of oval leaves 12-36 mm long and 6-22 mm broad. The orange, red or purple tubular flowers are 10-17 mm long, and are borne in pairs in the leaf axils. Often growing in colonies and spreading by means of an underground rootstock, it occurs in mixed bush on lower slopes or near streams from Worcester and Tulbagh to Swellendam. (Oct-Apr)

There are 4 species from the southwestern Cape to tropical Africa, of which 2 have been recorded in this area; *H. lucida*, the tree fuchsia, is a shrub or tree to 12 m.

Nemesia versicolor　　　　　　　　　　　　Leeubekkie　Weeskindertjies
An erect, simple or branched annual to 500 mm with oval, stalked, lower leaves and stalkless upper leaves 8-43 mm by 1-15 mm. The flowers are some 11 mm across, with a very short tube and a finger-like nectar-containing spur at the back as long as the petal lobes. It varies in colour from blue, mauve and yellow to white with upper and lower petals often dissimilar in colour, and the reverse often dark-veined. Occurring on sandy flats from Namaqualand to Knysna. (Aug-Nov)

There are about 65 species in southern and tropical Africa, 7 of which occur in this area.

Solanum guineense

Retzia capensis

Halleria elliptica

Nemesia versicolor

SCROPHULARIACEAE

Hyobanche sanguinea — Snail flower Katnaels Wolwekos
A leafless fleshy total parasite with an unbranched stem to 150 mm bearing crowded, velvety flowers 30-50 mm long. It is the curved anthers protruding from the flowers which give it the common name of "Katnaels".

There are about 7 species widespread in southern Africa, of which only this 1 is definitely recorded from this area. Another curious reddish leafless fleshy parasite, *Cytinus sanguineus* of the family *Rafflesiaceae,* resembling a budding snail flower from a distance, occurs in this area. It has massive separate male and female flowers enclosed within watermelon coloured bracts. *C. capensis* has purple-red bracts.

Melasma scabrum
A soft, partly parasitic, unbranched or sparsely-branched perennial to 1 m with pairs of lance-shaped, stalkless leaves up to 75 mm by 35 mm. The sweetly-scented funnel-shaped flowers are white or cream with a purple or brownish throat, and have 4 hairy stamens and a long, briefly-coiled slender style visible in the throat. Widespread as solitary plants throughout South Africa on marshy mountain slopes. There is only 1 species. (Nov-Mar)

Harveya capensis — Inkflower
A leafless totally parasitic branched or unbranched plant to 600 mm with a raceme of white or pinkish flowers. It has a hairy calyx with narrow lobes divided to about half-way, and wide-spreading petals up to 45 mm across which turn black if bruised. Found on mountain slopes from Namaqualand and throughout the Cape region to Port Elizabeth. (Oct-Feb)

There are about 40 species, mostly in Africa but some in Madagascar with 5 in this area: *H. tubulosa* is also pink or white, but has very short broad calyx lobes; *H. laxiflora* is rose-pink with paler markings and a narrow-lobed calyx; *H. purpurea* is purple or deep pink and *H. bolusii* has scarlet and yellow flowers.

Zaluzianskya capensis — Verfblommetjie
An erect slender usually hairy annual to 400 mm with narrow stalkless leaves up to 40 mm long. The extremely long-tubed flowers containing 4 stamens, emerge from a 2-lobed calyx which is slightly joined to the bract. Each flower is about 50 mm long and white with a red reverse. They remain tightly closed during the day and open late in the afternoon. Occurring on sand dunes or lower slopes from Namaqualand to the eastern Cape. (Apr-Dec)

There are some 40 species widespread in South Africa, of which 2 others have been recorded in this area.

Hyobanche sanguinea

Melasma scabrum

Harveya capensis

Zaluzianskya capensis

SCROPHULARIACEAE

Zaluzianskya villosa   Drumsticks
A densely-hairy or almost hairless sometimes sticky annual to 300 mm tall, branching from the base, with soft fleshy leaves. It bears a number of white or lilac often yellow-eyed flowers with a purple reverse. The corolla tube contains 2 stamens emerging from a 2-lobed calyx which is joined to the bract. Common on sandy flats and lower slopes from Namaqualand to this area and in the Karoo. (June-Nov)

Hemimeris racemosa
A weak-stemmed sticky-haired annual to 450 mm with square stems and pairs of delicate, oval, toothed leaves 6-25 mm by 2-15 mm. The flower buds, clothed with sticky glandular hairs, open into yellow flowers up to 16 mm across, growing singly in the leaf axils. The corolla is 2-lipped and slightly pouched at the base. There are 2 stamens. Occurring on sandy lower slopes and coastal flats from Namaqualand to Knysna. (July-Oct)

There are some 4 species in the Cape of which 2 occur in this area. The other, *H. sabulosa*, is almost hairless and has lobed leaves.

Sutera tristis
An erect finely-hairy glandular annual to 400 mm with oblong usually toothed leaves 25-60 mm by 5-30 mm. The flowers are borne in a spike of lime-green to yellowish flowers, with a long tube and 5 almost equal lobes; the upper 2 folding over the others in bud, and are strongly clove-scented at night. Common on sandy flats, slopes and dunes near the sea from Namibia to Mossel Bay. (Aug-Dec)

There are about 130 species in Africa and the Canary Isles, mostly in South Africa, of which 6 have been recorded in this area.

Manulea tomentosa
A densely-hairy sandpapery-textured perennial with sparsely-branched stems to 800mm, bearing stalked toothed leaves along their length. Each frosted flower, orange to brick-red in colour, has a short tube and 5 petal lobes which are folded along their length to resemble short fat fingers, the upper 2 folding over the others in bud. Found on sand dunes and lower slopes from the Cape Peninsula to Bredasdorp. (June-Dec)

There are about 60 species, mostly in South Africa, with 5 in this area. Two others with yellowish-orange flowers are *M. cheiranthus* with a basal rosette of broad leaves and very long thin spidery petal lobes; and the profusely-branched *M. leiostachys* with very narrow leaves.

Zaluzianskya villosa

Hemimeris racemosa

Sutera tristis

Manulea tomentosa

SCROPHULARIACEAE

Teedia lucida Stinkbos
A pungent-scented hairless sprawling shrub to 1,2 m with square branched stems and pairs of oval leaves up to 150 mm by 50 mm, but usually less. Clusters of purplish or mauve flowers 15 mm long are followed by drab purple or yellowish-brown berries. Occurring as isolated plants on mountain slopes often in shade or among rocks from Namaqualand throughout the southern Cape to Natal. (Sept-Jan)
 There are 2 species confined to South Africa, of which only this 1 occurs in this area.

Manulea minor
A common but usually insignificant annual to 300 mm, single-stemmed or branched from the base. It has a basal rosette of shallowly-toothed oval leaves, and bears heads of tiny white flowers with short broad lobes and 4 stamens. The heads elongate as the flowers mature. Found in sand on lower slopes and flats throughout this area. (July-Nov)

SELAGINACEAE

Agathelpis dubia Cat's Tail
A soft sparingly-branched perennial to 600 mm becoming woody at the base, with very narrow crowded hairless leaves 6-18 mm long. The flowers arise singly from dull-coloured bracts, 4-5 mm long, which hide the tubular 5-lobed calyx. The tubular curved corolla with 5 small lobes may be pale yellow or deep red-brown and has a penetratingly sweet scent at night. Occurring on flats and slopes from the Gifberg to the Cape Peninsula and into the Caledon district. (May-Dec)

Dischisma ciliatum
An erect spreading annual or perennial, with densely-leafy sparsely-branched stems to 400 mm. It has narrow toothed leaves 6-25 mm long, and 8-16 mm long flowers in dense spikes. The corolla has 4 lobes slit in front to resemble a small open upstanding hand. Occurring on slopes and flats from Nieuwoudtville to Port Elizabeth and the Karoo. (Aug-Dec)
 There are 11 species in southern Africa of which 2 others occur in this area: the sparsely-leafy and much-branched greenish-flowered *D. arenarium* of dunes and flats; and *D. capitatum* with rounded heads of whitish flowers nestling in a rosette of long leaves. The very similar genus *Hebenstreitia*, represented by 5 species in this area, has what appear to be 1 large outer and 1 small inner 'calyx lobe'.

Teedia lucida

Manulea minor

Agathelpis dubia

Dischisma ciliatum

SELAGINACEAE

Selago serrata — Blouaarbossie
An erect or sprawling shrublet with stout angular branches to 900 mm and crowded recurved hairless leaves about 12-25 mm by 5-10 mm. The flowers are in dense heads up to 100 mm across. At fruiting time the heads elongate into structures resembling very long, thin, heads of barley. Widespread on mountain slopes from Clanwilliam to Knysna. (Oct-Feb)

There are more than 150 species in Africa, of which at least 6 have been recorded in this area. Two more have broadish leaves: the upright mauve or purple *S. verbenacea* with profusely-branched stems; and the delicate *S. incisa* of the west of this area with white, cream or pale blue flowers, which becomes abundant after veld fires.

Selago spuria — Bergaarbossie
An annual or perennial branched at the base with stems to 600 mm and clearly toothed leaves 5-30 mm long and only 1-3 mm wide. The flowers may be purple, lilac, pink or white in heads 5-15 mm across, often aggregated into loose or dense clusters up to 90 mm across. After flowering they elongate into narrow tightly packed fruiting heads up to 110 mm long. Common and widespread at all altitudes from Gifberg to Uniondale. (Oct-Jan)

Two others have equally narrow leaves but the edges are not toothed: the pale mauve-flowered, soft-leaved *S. thunbergii*; and the white-flowered, harsh-leaved *S. scabrida* of the west of this area.

DIPSACACEAE

Scabiosa columbaria — Bitterbos Scabious
A rather soft perennial to 800 mm with variable toothed or deeply-cut leaves up to 100 mm long, and flowerheads to 50 mm across on long stalks. Occurring on sandy flats and slopes from the southwestern Cape to the eastern Cape and north to the Transvaal; it is also found in Europe and Asia. (Aug-Feb)

There are about 100 species in the Old World and 9 in South Africa, of which this is probably the only representative in this area.

CAMPANULACEAE

Lobelia jasionoides
A low-growing mat-forming annual with almost hairless leaves 10-22 mm by 1-10 mm (broadest in shady places), and lilac and white flowers grouped into crowded heads. The corolla is split down the back with the column of stamens arching through. Occurring at upper altitudes from Vanrhynsdorp to Swellendam. (Oct-Feb)

There are about 300 species worldwide with some 18 in this area.

Selago serrata

Selago spuria

Scabiosa columbaria

Lobelia jasionoides

CAMPANULACEAE

Cyphia volubilis Aardboontjie Bergbaroe
A slender twiner with stems to 750 mm, and simple leaves up to 55 mm long by 3 mm broad. The irregular flowers are variable in colour and may be blue, purple, mauve, pink or white. Occurring from sea level to the upper mountain slopes from Namaqualand to the Outeniquas. (Aug-Oct)

There are about 50 species, mainly southern African, with at least 5 in this area. Another twining species, *C. digitata*, has lobed leaves.

Cyphia bulbosa Bergbaroe
A geophyte with annual unbranched or sparsely-branched leafy stems to 400 mm with deeply lobed leaves basically triangular in shape, decreasing in size upwards, the longest being 50-60 mm long. The irregular flowers are 7-10 mm long. Common on flats and slopes from Clanwilliam along the coastal belt to the eastern Cape. It is most noticeable after veld fires. (Aug-Oct)

Another non-twining species is *C. phyteuma*, with lilac flowers and a basal tuft of leaves.

Lobelia pubescens
A soft sprawling perennial with spoon-shaped irregularly-toothed leaves; the lower are up to 20 mm long, becoming progressively smaller and narrower upwards along the stem. The white or pale blue flowers, which may have blue or white markings respectively, are 11-17 mm long and have narrow petal lobes which are very delicately hairy. It occurs from Tulbagh and the Cape Peninsula to Humansdorp, often in shady places or sprawling on damp rocks. It blooms throughout the year.

This is one of a group of soft sprawling plants found in sheltered dampish places with minor technical distinguishing characteristics.

Lobelia chamaepitys Wild lobelia
A perennial with a simple or branched densely leafy stem, the leaves being narrow, toothed and about 20 mm long. The leafless wiry flowering stems are light brown in colour, with 1 or 2 bright violet blue hairless flowers 10-16 mm long. As in all lobelias the corolla is split down the back with the column of stamens arching through. Frequent on mountain slopes from Stellenbosch to Swellendam. (Sept-Apr)

Three other very similar species occur in this area: the purple-blue and white, occasionally pink *L. coronopifolia* has green flowering stems; two have hairy flowers; *L. tomentosa* has harshly hairy leaves; and *L. linearis* has threadlike much-divided leaves.

Cyphia volubilis

Cyphia bulbosa

Lobelia pubescens

Lobelia chamaepitys

CAMPANULACEAE

Lobelia setacea
A diffuse soft plant branched mainly at the base, with thin intertwined stems scarcely more than 1 mm thick. The plant appears leafless because the narrowness of the 5-15 mm long leaves makes them look like thin side-branches. The flowers are 8-12 mm long, comparatively small for the genus, with a rather broad lower lip. The steely blue colour is distinctive. Occurring on sandy flats from Worcester to Caledon. (Nov-Apr)

Lightfootia diffusa
A stiff erect or sprawling shrublet to 500 mm with tufts of tiny recurved leaves. The regular white, blue or purple flowers, usually in 3's are 5-8 mm long with narrow petal lobes typically free almost to the base. Common on damp lower slopes and along the coast from Worcester and Stellenbosch to the eastern Cape. (Oct-May)

There are about 60 species in tropical and South Africa, and Madagascar, of which some 8 occur in this area.

Merciera leptoloba
A woody perennial resprouting after veld fires, with sprawling stems to 300 mm and crowded narrow leaves to 20 mm long. The tips of the stems curve upwards to display a short spike of curry-scented white flowers with a style which does not project beyond the petals. Occurring on lower to mid-slopes, especially in disturbed places, in the Caledon district. (Dec-Feb)

There are 5 species all confined to the fynbos, and all recorded in this area. Another white-flowered species, *M. brevifolia* is distinguished by having leaves less than 15 mm long, and a style which projects well beyond the petals.

Merciera tenuifolia
A sprawling, much-branched shrublet with branches to 300 mm resprouting after veld fires, with crowded rough bristly leaves 10-30 mm long. The sessile violet-purple or blue-purple flowers arise among the leaves and are for the most part considerably longer. It occurs in sandy or rocky places at medium altitudes on mountains from Tulbagh to Hermanus. (Dec-Mar)

Other species are *M. eckloniana*, with deep violet flowers and leaves less than 10 mm long, and the rare pinkish-purple high-altitude *M. vaginata* with projecting stamens.

Lobelia setacea

Lightfootia diffusa

Merciera leptoloba

Merciera tenuifolia

CAMPANULACEAE

Roella arenaria
A sprawling irregularly-branched shrublet to 400 mm with rough-textured crowded narrow leaves 5-10 mm long. The single terminal flowers emerge from scaly bracts which curve sharply backwards, and have pale blue or white sharp-pointed petals to 15 mm long. The calyx lobes are hairy on the outside. Occurring on sandy soils on the coastal plain from the Palmiet River to near Cape Agulhas. (Dec)

There are about 25 species from the southwestern Cape to Natal, of which 10 occur in this area.

Roella incurva
A woody usually erect branched perennial with white-hairy stems to 600 mm and crowded tufts of incurved narrow leaves to about 8 mm, which soon turn brown, with comb-like teeth at the edge near the tip. The regular flowers, usually dark-spotted within, are 15-25 mm long and have pointed petals. Solitary or in groups of 2 or 3, they emerge from a bulging cluster of greenish leaf-like bracts and longer broader sepals, coarsely brown-toothed on the edges. Common and widespread on the lower mountain slopes from Tulbagh to Swellendam. (Oct-Jan)

Two more species in this area have flowers 15 mm long or more, commonly with dark spots: *R. ciliata* has rounded petals and bracts with coarse white bristles; and the sprawling *R. maculata* has bracts and sepals covered with felt-like hairs.

Roella prostrata
A woody-stemmed prostrate or erect branched shrublet to 500 mm with tufted leaves up to 10 mm long, white-hairy towards the base. The single regular flowers, 8-13 mm long, arise among rather crowded leaflike bracts which may be toothed and have a hairless calyx. The petals are white or pale blue without markings. Occurring on the coastal flats from Malmesbury to Caledon. (Dec-Apr)

Siphocodon debilis
A tangled wiry harsh-textured shrublet to 350 mm with green, arching flowering branches. The leaves are reduced to 1-2 mm long scales, and the white or pale blue almost sessile regular flowers, perhaps 8 mm long, are borne on angled branch tips and open towards midday. Found scattered in low fynbos on stony or sandy lower mountain slopes from the Onrus mountains to Hermanus. (Jan-Apr)

Another very much finer form occurs in tangled heaps in damp, shady places or sloping marshes at high altitude. There are 2 species, *S. spartioides* being a sparser coarser shrublet with erect flowering branches.

Roella arenaria

Roella incurva

Roella prostrata

Siphocodon debilis

CAMPANULACEAE

Prismatocarpus diffusus
A dainty tufted shrublet to 450 mm, resprouting after veld fires with woody, leafy basal parts bearing narrow leaves up to 15 mm by 3 mm. The 13 mm long violet or white sessile flowers have a short tube with the petals abruptly reflexed to display 5 free stamens and a style longer than the corolla. Occurring on rocky mountain slopes from Piketberg and Worcester to Caledon. (Nov-Feb)

There are 31 species, mainly South African but 1 extending into the tropics, with 10 having been recorded in this area. No others have reflexed petals and long styles.

Monopsis lutea   Yellow lobelia
A straggling bristly perennial with narrow leaves borne on thin stems to 600 mm long. The hairy sulphur-yellow flowers, like those of *Lobelia*, are 2-lipped and split down the back, but differ in forming a funnel-shaped tube. Occurring on damp flats and lower slopes from Clanwilliam to the Peninsula and Caledon to Riversdale and the western Karoo. (Nov-Apr)

There are about 18 species in tropical and South Africa, with 2 in this area. The annual *M. simplex* is a tufted shrublet with purple flowers.

ASTERACEAE

Senecio elegans   Wild cineraria   Strandblommetjie
An annual to 1 m tall with variable leaves 35-75 mm long with rounded or finely divided lobes. They are often somewhat clammy to the touch, those plants growing on the seashore being slightly fleshy. The flowerheads are 25 mm across and are clasped below by 2 rows of smooth green bracts with brown tips. A very common and colourful constituent of sandy coastal flats and lower slopes, found from Namaqualand to the eastern Cape. (July-Mar)

There are over 2 000 species worldwide with about 250 in South Africa and 22 in this area. Another purple-flowered species of the seashore is *S. arenarius*, which has hairy bracts.

Disparago lasiocarpa
A densely-leafy sometimes woody shrublet to 300 mm with slightly twisted needle-like leaves to 6 mm long. The flowers form dense, rounded clusters of flowerheads up to 14 mm in diameter, pinkish or purplish in colour, and are in pairs between dry papery bracts. It is widespread in sandy and stony places at low and medium altitudes from Piketberg to Riversdale. (Nov-Feb)

Seven species are found in South Africa, mostly in the fynbos, with 4 in this area. They are distinguishable on microscopic characters only.

Prismatocarpus diffusus

Monopsis lutea

Senecio elegans

Disparago lasiocarpa

ASTERACEAE

Gazania pectinata
A soft perennial to 200 mm with tufts of short-stalked leaves. They may be narrow and strap-like or pinnately divided (sometimes on the same plant), green and smooth or bristly above, and pale and woolly below. The solitary yellow or orange flowerheads are borne on hairy stalks up to 300 mm long and are up to 90 mm across. They arise from a firm, smooth or bristly cup of several rows of bracts, the innermost slightly papery-edged, all joined for less than half their length. Occurring commonly in sand or fine gravel soils at low altitudes. (Aug-Nov)

There are about 16 species in Africa, of which 5 occur in this area. The common and widespread *G. krebsiana* has flowerstalks rarely longer than 150 mm and the bracts are non-hairy.

Corymbium africanum   Heuningbossie   Plampers
A perennial to 300 mm with a tuft of very narrow harsh leaves up to 200 mm long. The flowers are grouped together in flat heads and may be purple, pink or white, each with 5 sticky bracts, the inner 2 longer than the outer. It is found on flats and mountains from the Cedarberg to the Langkloof and Swartberg and blooms especially profusely after veld fires. (Oct-Jan)

There are 7 species confined to the fynbos area.

Corymbium villosum   Heuningbossie
A perennial with harshly hairy basal leaves 100-150 mm long and about 10 mm wide. Bristly flowering stems up to 300 mm bear flat heads of white or mauve flowers which emerge from bracts half the length of the flowers. Occurring on lower slopes from the Cedarberg to Swellendam. (Sept-Nov)

Another hairy species, *C. congestum*, has sandpapery harsh stems, leaves 15-25 mm wide, and inner bracts as long as the flowers.

Pteronia camphorata   Gombos   Ghombossie
A much-branched, twiggy, aromatic shrub to 1 m or more with rough white-hairy stems and hairless needlelike leaves 10-13 mm long. The single or loosely-clustered heads are raised above the leaves and surrounded by several rows of overlapping bracts with papery edges. Occurring from the coast to the upper slopes from Namaqualand to Piketberg and the Cape Peninsula to Bredasdorp. (Aug-Dec)

There are 75 species mostly in the Cape Province, of which 4 occur in this area. The other 3 have thistle-like heads with broad bracts enfolding the flowers in a tight rounded head: the bristly *P. hirsuta* has pink flowers; the sand-papery *P. scabra* has orange flowers; and the hairless, smooth, *P. tenuifolia* has golden flowers and densely knobbly-warted leaves.

Gazania pectinata　　　　　　　*Corymbium africanum*

Corymbium villosum　　　　　　*Pteronia camphorata*

ASTERACEAE

Phaenocoma prolifera   Everlasting   Rooisewejaartjie
An erect, stiffly-branched woody shrub to 600 mm with scale-like leaves. The large showy flowerheads have glistening papery 'petals', which are in fact bracts, surrounding the tiny flowers within. They gradually fade with age, remaining on the plants for many months. Occurring in coastal or mountain fynbos from Ceres, Worcester, Ladismith and the Cape Peninsula to Bredasdorp. (Sept-Apr)
    There is only 1 species.

Helichrysum vestitum   Sewejaartjie   Tontelblom
A robust, much-branched woolly shrub to 1 m, with narrow crowded leaves 800 mm or more in length, becoming smaller towards the top of the plant. The flowerheads are borne singly on white woolly stalks with dry membranous bracts becoming more crowded towards the top. The tiny purplish flowers in the centre are surrounded by several rows of papery white pointed bracts, each head being about 50 mm across and 35 mm long. Quite common on the flats and middle slopes from Paarl and the Cape Peninsula to Knysna and on the Swartberg mountains. (Nov-Jan)
    There are over 500 species in Africa, southern Europe, Asia and Australia with about 27 in this area.

Helichrysum retortum
A straggling, sand-binding shrublet with stems to 450 mm long, rooting at intervals. The silvery leaves are 11-30 mm by 2-6 mm. Solitary flowerheads varying from 40 to 80 mm across are borne on short erect branchlets. Occurring never far from the sea on cliffs, dunes or flats from the Cape Peninsula to Riversdale. (Aug-Dec)
    H. stoloniferum of the Franschhoek mountains is similar but half the size.

Edmondia pinifolia
A loose shrublet to 250 mm, with many slender stems from the base, resprouting after fire. The leaves are unusual in that they are woolly-white above and smooth and green below. They are crowded, needlelike and up to 25 mm long on the lower parts, gradually becoming smaller on the flower-bearing branches. The single strawberry-pink or bone-coloured flowerheads can be up to 50 mm across, with papery bracts. Occurring on steep, rocky, often moist slopes at medium to high altitudes from the Cape Peninsula to Swellendam. (Sept-Feb)
    There are 3 species, with 2 occurring in this area.

Phaenocoma prolifera

Helichrysum vestitum

Helichrysum retortum

Edmondia pinifolia

ASTERACEAE

Felicia tenella
A dainty annual to 200 mm with simple ericoid leaves up to 25 mm long. The flowerheads are about 10 mm across and may be pink, pale blue or mauve. They are borne singly on almost leafless unbranched stalks. It is found in moist sandy areas on flats or coastal dunes from Nieuwoudtville to Riversdale and flowers throughout the year.
  There are about 83 species, all African, with 7 in this area.

Ursinia eckloniana
A robust, single-stemmed shrub to 1,2 m with flat, overlapping leaves 37-50 mm by 6-10 mm, confined to the upper part of the stem. The single flowerheads 30-50 mm across, arise in the axils of the upper leaves and are enfolded below by 5-6 rows of greenish bracts with dark edges, the innermost longest with golden papery tips. Occurring on mountain slopes from Paarl to Caledon. (July-Apr)
  There are 40 species, all except 1 in South Africa, with 13 in this area. The rather similar swamp-loving *U. caledonica*, has flowerheads arising at the branch tips, and smaller leaves.

Ursinia quinquepartita
An erect, single-stemmed shrublet to 400 mm, the upper stems densely-leafy, the lower parts with persistent flattened leafstalks. Each stem has a single flowerhead, enfolded below by 5 rows of dark-edged bracts, the innermost tipped with large papery flaps. Occurring most frequently in damp places on mountains from Stellenbosch to Caledon. (Nov-Apr)

Ursinia paleacea   Geelmargriet
An erect almost hairless perennial to 900 mm, branched at the base, with leaves 20-60 mm long, divided into long narrow segments. Slender, relatively leafless stems are gracefully arched over in bud, straightening as the flowerhead opens. There are 6-7 rows of bracts, the innermost longest with very pronounced papery tips. It is common on damp mountain slopes from Tulbagh to the Cape Peninsula and eastwards to Humansdorp. (Oct-Feb)

Felicia tenella

Ursinia eckloniana

Ursinia quinquepartita

Ursinia paleacea

ASTERACEAE

Haplocarpha lanata Brandbossie
A perennial with basal leaves sometimes 200 mm long, but often less, sandpapery in texture above and pale and felt-like below. The single flowerheads are borne on leafless woolly stalks about 150 mm long, arising from among the leaves at ground level. They are surrounded by many rows of free bracts, the outer small and leafy, the inner rounded and membranous. The white or yellow flowerheads with red or purple reverse can be up to 35 mm across. It occurs throughout this area and is most frequently observed in recently burnt veld. (Mar-June)
   There are 8 species in Africa, of which only 1 occurs in this area.

Thaminophyllum latifolium
An aromatic, straggling shrublet to 750 mm with silky branches and silky sessile leaves, 7-10 mm long, which become bald and rough with age. The flowerheads are about 24 mm across on short stalks, and are white or pink with a pink-purple reverse. Occurring on south-facing slopes, often in damp places, on the Klein River mountains. (Aug-Dec)
   There are 3 species all found in this area. All have rather wide, well-spaced rounded "petals".

Polyarrhena reflexa Wilde aster
Superficially very similar to the previous species, this is a straggling, bristly undershrub to 1 m with broad-based, recurving leaves about 10 mm by 4 mm with barbed edges. The single flowerheads, about 18 mm across, are white above and reddish on the reverse. It forms large dense mats especially in moist places on the lower slopes, and occurs from Paarl and the Cape Peninsula to Caledon. (June-Sept)
   There are 4 species, all confined to the southwestern Cape of which 1 other, *O. stricta,* occurs in this area; it is distinguished by its straight, not recurved, leaves.

Othonna dentata
A succulent shrub with thick fleshy partly-woody stems. The leaves, borne towards the tips of the branches, are 37-50 mm long and half as wide, with edges which may be quite smooth to sharply or coarsely toothed. It has 1 or more branched almost leafless flowering stems bearing heads about 20 mm across, with a single row of joined bracts shorter than the flowers within. Occurring in fissures in rocks on mountain slopes from the Cape Peninsula to Hermanus. (May-Dec)
   There are about 145 species in South Africa, of which 5 have been recorded from this area. *O. parviflora* has oval leaves all the way up the stem and flowerheads in dense clusters up to 180 mm across.

Haplocarpha lanata

Thaminophyllum latifolium

Polyarrhena reflexa

Othonna dentata

ASTERACEAE

Othonna quinquedentata
An erect shrub to 2 m, single-stemmed or sparsely-branched from near the base, with the lower stems becoming woody with age. The slightly fleshy leaves are clustered untidily on the lower stems and are often streaked and spotted with red. They are 50-150 mm by 10-50 mm, broadest in the upper half, often with a toothed edge. The flowerheads are borne on almost leafless branched stems, each up to 30 mm across, and have a single row of joined bracts shorter than the flowers. Occurring in damp places on lower slopes and flats from Worcester and the Cape Peninsula to Mossel Bay and the Swartberg mountains; it becomes abundant as a pioneer plant in disturbed places, especially after veld fires. (Jan-Dec)

Osmitopsis parvifolia
A hairless shrublet to 400 mm with crowded, toothed leaves, neatly spiralled up the stem, clearly smaller towards the top. The flowerheads, 20-25 mm across, are borne singly at the ends of the branches and are surrounded by several rows of soft green bracts. Occurring among rocks on mid and upper slopes from Sir Lowry's Pass to Kleinmond. (Sept-Feb)

There are 9 species in the western Cape of which 6 occur in this area.

Osmitopsis asteriscoides   Mountain daisy   Belskruie
A slender leggy camphor-scented shrub to 2 m with lower stems leafless, exposing the cracked naked bark. The upper stems are well branched, with crowded velvety leaves up to 80 mm by 18 mm. The flowerheads are about 35 mm across and borne on short side branches, but not at the tip of the main stem. It occurs, often in dense stands, in open sunny swamps and seepage areas from Paarl to Caledon. (Jan-Dec)

Chrysanthemoides monilifera   Boneseed bush (Australia)   Bietou Boetabessie
A dense shrub to 2 m with leaves up to 45 mm by 25 mm with a smooth or toothed edge. The flowerhead is 20 mm across, and the fruit is a purple berry, which distinguishes this species from nearly all other daisies. The berries are beloved by birds and the seeds are widely dispersed in their droppings. It grows in the coastal districts from the southwestern Cape to the eastern Cape and on to tropical Africa, and flowers all the year round. It has also been introduced into Australia and America and in the former country it has become a serious pest plant, invading huge areas of natural vegetation.

There are 2 species; the other, *C. incana*, a straggling shrub of coastal dunes and inland sandy slopes, is spiny and grey-leaved.

Othonna quinquedentata

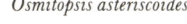

Osmitopsis parvifolia

Osmitopsis asteriscoides

Chrysanthemoides monilifera

ASTERACEAE

Metalasia muricata　　　　　　　　　　　　　Blombos　Witsteekbossie
A variable much-branched shrub to 2 m, with tufts of needlelike twisted leaves 6-18 mm long with a woolly upper and woolly or naked lower surface. The numerous flowerheads are surrounded by several tightly-enfolding rows of bracts, the outer brown-tipped and the inner white or pink, all clustered rather loosely on a much-branched flowerhead stalk. It is widespread in the western to eastern Cape mainly in the coastal areas and in the Transvaal and Lesotho. At higher altitudes a much more slender form with a few open branches is found.

There are about 33 species in South Africa and some 12 in this area.

Metalasia muricata
A pink-flowered form with ericoid leaves, found on sandy flats at Kleinmond, which illustrates the variability of the species. (Jan-Dec)

Metalasia cephalotes　　　　　　　　　　　　　　　　　　　Rooiblombossie
A variable stiffly-branched erect or spreading shrub to 1 m with matted-woolly branches and slightly twisted needlelike leaves up to 10 mm long, borne singly or in tufts. The flowerheads have several rows of white or pink bracts tangled together with matted wool. Occurring on flats and mountain slopes throughout this area and from Worcester to Bredasdorp. (Aug-Mar)

This is the only species with a matted head.

Castalis nudicaulis　　　　　　　　　　Ox-eye daisy　Wilde margriet
A perennial with variable, usually toothed, leaves 100 mm long by 15 mm wide, crowded at the base of the stem. The flowerheads are about 60 mm across, borne singly on a harsh leafless hairy stem. They are white with a purple or coppery reverse. It is quite common on mountain slopes from Clanwilliam to Uniondale. (Aug-Sept)

There are 3 species in South Africa, 2 confined to the fynbos, of which this is the sole representative in this area.

Metalasia muricata

Metalasia muricata

Metalasia cephalotes

Castalis nudicaulis

ASTERACEAE

Oedera capensis
A straggling prickly shrublet to 300 mm, with rather rigid narrow leaves about 15-25 mm long, with short spines. Terminal flowerheads up to 35 mm across are surrounded by a few rows of bracts, the outer leafy and inner translucent. Occurring commonly on dry flats and slopes from the Cape Peninsula and Robertson to the eastern Cape. (June-Dec)

There are 6 species confined to the fynbos, of which only 2 occur in this area.

Oedera imbricata
A stiff erect rather harsh prickly shrublet to 300 mm with almost hairless recurved leaves with minute teeth on the edges. The yellow to orange flowerheads are up to 50 mm across, often in groups at the ends of the stems. It is found on flats and mountains from Malmesbury to George. (Aug-Nov)

Osteospermum tomentosum
A dwarf perennial with tufts of spoon-shaped leaves up to 45 mm long by 25 mm broad, smooth above and pale woolly below. The flowerheads, up to 25 mm across, are borne on long stalks with sparse, very dwarf leaves. Occurring on the lower and mid-slopes from Tulbagh to Mossel Bay, it resprouts and blooms very quickly after veld fires. (Sept-Apr)

Osteospermum rotundifolium
An erect rather leggy, sparsely-branched shrub to 2 m with tufts of cotton wool in the axils of the leaves. The alternate, sessile bluegreen leaves 10-30 mm by 5-25 mm, have a point at the tip. The unbranched or branched flowerhead stalks are densely clothed with glandular hairs as are the soft green bracts. Occurring on the slopes of the Klein River mountains. (Oct-Dec)

There are about 70 species, mainly African, of which some 14 occur in this area. *O. polygaloides* is superficially identical but occurs throughout the area except for the Klein River mountains.

Oedera capensis

Oedera imbricata

Osteospermum tomentosum

Osteospermum rotundifolium

ASTERACEAE

Felicia aethiopica
Wilde aster

A dense leafy shrublet to 500 mm or more, often rooting at the nodes, with harsh oval to tongue-shaped almost sessile leaves 2-5 mm wide. The blue flowerheads with a yellow eye, some 30 mm across, are carried well above the foliage on long harsh-textured naked stalks. They have a single row of free bracts. Occurring on flats from the Cedarberg to the eastern Cape and Natal. (Jan-Dec)

Gerbera tomentosa
Tontelblaarbossie

A perennial with a tuft of leathery leaves at ground level, up to 200 mm long and 50 mm wide. They are at first covered with dense woolly hairs, but the upper surface becomes bald and glossy green later. The ivory-coloured flowerheads, about 80 mm across, are borne singly on almost leafless, ivory-hairy stems up to 600 mm tall. Occasional on dry stony southfacing slopes from Paarl to Bredasdorp; it blooms mostly after veld fires. (Jan-Dec)

There are about 100 species in Africa and Asia with about 30 in South Africa and 4 in this area. *G. linnaei* has leathery, much-lobed leaves; *G. crocea* has leaves similar to *G. tomentosa*, but cobwebby scaly flowerhead stems; and *G. piloselloides* has flowers half the size and leaves with very short stalks.

Oldenbergia paradoxa

A hard, cushion-forming shrublet, from a thick woody rootstock. The stiff darkgreen leaves are woolly underneath, 50-60 mm long by 6-12 mm wide. Creamcoloured, stalkless, thistlelike flowerheads some 50 mm across nestle among the leaves. Only buds can be seen on the specimen in the illustration. It is rather rare in rock crevices at high altitudes in this area. (Jan-July)

There are 4 species in the southwestern to eastern Cape with only 1 other, *O. intermedia*, with long-stalked flowerheads, occurring in this area.

Mairea corymbosa

A soft-stemmed shrublet to about 600 mm with narrow 3-ribbed leaves 25-38 mm long. The flowerheads may be blue, mauve, pink or white and are borne on sandpapery stems with small bracts at intervals. The heads are about 20 mm across, with a few rows of loose hairy green pointed bracts below. It occurs on mountain slopes, usually near streams, in the Caledon district. (July-Sept)

There are 14 species in the southwestern and south Cape, about 8 occurring in this area.

Felicia aethiopica

Gerbera tomentosa

Oldenbergia paradoxa

Mairea corymbosa

ASTERACEAE

Edmondia sesamoides Everlasting Sewejaartjie
Strooiblommetjie

A single-stemmed shrublet with a few open branches, reaching about 500 mm in height. The narrow leaves clasp the stem tightly, with an abrupt transition between the lowest leaves, those on the flowering stalks and the bracts around the flowers. The flowerheads, borne singly at the tips of the branches are ruby-red in bud, opening yellow or sometimes white or pink. It occurs on rocky flats and slopes from Paarl to Riversdale. (Aug-Jan)

Helipterum zeyheri

A sturdy shrublet to 200 mm, with upright stems closely clothed with rather narrow felt-textured leaves up to 50 mm by 6-8 mm, becoming smaller upwards. The stems below the flowers bear small scattered rosy bracts which become larger and more crowded at the base of the flowerhead. The colour fades to white as the flowers opens. Occurring from the Cape Peninsula to Hermanus on grassy and rocky flats and slopes. (Aug-Oct)

There are about 97 species in South Africa and Australia, with perhaps 9 in this area.

Helichrysum felinum Strawberry everlasting

A slender perennial to 1 m, woody and single-stemmed below, sparsely-branched and densely leafy above. The leaves are woolly and cobwebby at first, later becoming bald and the upper surface is harsh to the touch like a chameleon's skin. The flowerheads are enclosed in crinkled papery bracts, usually reddish and looking like little strawberries in bud, but sometimes milk-white. They fade to white as the flowers open, revealing the yellow centres. Each head is only 6-10 mm across, borne in clusters at the tips of the branches. Occurring on rocky slopes from the Cape Peninsula and Worcester east to Natal along the coastal belt. (Sept-Dec)

Helichrysum foetidum Stinksewejaartjie

A foetid-smelling, stout, simple or sparingly branched biennial to 1 m. In the first year the leaves form a rosette at ground level, which withers as the flowering stems emerge in the second year. They then produce lance-shaped, sessile leaves 40-90 mm by 10-25 mm, becoming smaller upwards. A large cluster of flat-topped 15-25 mm heads, surrounded by 8-9 rows of glossy yellow or cream bracts much longer than the flowers, appears at the top. Occurring on hill and mountain slopes especially in damp places along streams or forest margins from the Cedarberg, Worcester, and the Cape Peninsula to the Transkei, along the coastal belt. (Oct-May)

Edmondia sesamoides

Helipterum zeyheri

Helichrysum felinum

Helichrysum foetidum

ASTERACEAE

Gymnodiscus capillaris
A small hairless annual with tufts of succulent lobed or unlobed leaves about 60 mm by 15 mm, or often less. Flowering stems up to 200 mm bear clusters of tiny flowerheads each only 3 mm across, with a single layer of broad bracts joined only at the base. Occurring on sandy flats and lower slopes from Namaqualand and the western Karoo to Mossel Bay. (June-Oct)

There are 2 species in South Africa, of which only this occurs in this area.

Heterolepis aliena
A spreading rounded shrub to 600 mm high and more across, with crowded narrow leaves 25-37 mm long. The edges are rolled under, nearly concealing the pale woolly lower surface. Flowerheads about 60 mm across on sand-papery leafless stalks often cover the plant, obscuring the leaves. It occurs on rocky slopes and in crevices from the Cedarberg southwards and throughout this area. (Sept-Jan)

There are 3 species in the southwestern Cape, of which 1 other, *H. peduncularis*, occurs in the drier parts of this area. It has flowerheads 30 mm across on stalks 60-100 mm long and less crowded leaves.

Euryops abrotanifolius   Geel margriet
A robust erect shrub to 2 m, single-stemmed or with a few branches at the top. The leathery to slightly fleshy leaves are blueish-green, usually crowded, up to 90 mm long, with the segments scarcely 1,5 mm wide. The solitary, occasionally clustered, flowerheads, 30-50 mm across, are sometimes reddish on the reverse and have a single row of bracts united into a smooth cup. This typical member of the fynbos, found from Calvinia to Riversdale on sandy and rocky slopes, from sea-level to 1800 m is often a pioneer after veld fires. (Jan-Dec)

There are about 100 species in Africa, with 4 in this area.

Berkheya barbata
A rather rigid erect shrublet to 600 mm with the spiny leaves characteristic of the genus arranged in pairs. They are dark above but strikingly paler and woolly below, up to 60 mm long and 25 mm broad. The flowerheads, up to 100 mm in diameter are surrounded by several rows of long spiny leaflike bracts. It is found from the coast to the lower coastal mountain slopes, from Gifberg to Bredasdorp. (Aug-Jan)

There are about 150 species, mostly in Africa, with 2 others in this area. *B. herbacea*, with rather smaller clustered flowerheads and alternate leaves, up to 200 mm by 50 mm wide; and *B. rigida*, with clusters of very many flowerheads not more than 35 mm across, and alternate, much-divided leaves some 8 mm wide.

Gymnodiscus capillaris *Heterolepis aliena*

Euryops abrotanifolius *Berkheya barbata*

ASTERACEAE

Hippia frutescens   Rankals
An aromatic, erect or straggling, weakly-branched shrub to 600 mm with hairy branches bearing rather crowded, pinnately-divided leaves up to 60 mm long. The flowerheads, each seldom more than 6 mm across, are grouped in dense or open clusters at the ends of the branches, and are surrounded by 2 rows of green bracts with papery edges. Occurring from sea level to 2000 m from Piketberg along the Cape mountains to Uitenhage and also in the Transvaal. (Aug-Jan)

There are 7 species in South Africa, mostly in the fynbos regions of which 3 have been recorded in this area.

Senecio triqueter
A hairless sparsely-branched shrublet to 300 mm with leafy branches bearing needlelike leaves 8-15 mm long. Leafless stems arise at the tips, bearing single heads about 18 mm across. They are enfolded below by a double circle of greenish bracts, the length of the inner approximately double that of the outer and alternately papery-edged. Occurring on slopes from the Cape Peninsula to Caledon. (Jan-May)

S. pinifolius, with rather longer leaves and a circle of yellow ray florets, is the only similar species.

Stoebe incana
An erect, greyish, rounded shrub to 500 mm with threadlike, spirally-twisted leaves usually less than 6 mm long and woolly when young. It bears groups of elongated or rounded loosely-packed glistening golden heads, each tiny head containing 1 flower. Occurring on slopes and ridges on the mountains from Paarl and the Cape Peninsula to Caledon. (Feb-May)

There are 34 species in southern and tropical Africa, with 11 in this area. *S. cinerea* is very similar to *S. incana*, except that the leaves have basal lumps visible to a sharp eye, borne on branches of different lengths and thicknesses; the latter characteristic is shared by *S. plumosa*, the grey-white slangbos, with 1 mm long leaves in tufts.

Athanasia parviflora
A sturdy densely leafy shrub to 1,3 m with pinnately-branched needlelike leaves up to 70 mm long. The flowerheads, emerging from slender branches among the uppermost leaves, can be 100 mm across. Each head is made up of a multitude of flower clusters each 5 mm long by 1-2 mm wide, and surrounded by many rows of horny bracts. The flowers have a strong sickly-sweet scent. The species is widespread on flats and mountains from Namaqualand to Uitenhage. (Nov-Dec)

Hippia frutescens

Senecio triqueter

Stoebe incana

Athanasia parviflora

ASTERACEAE

Senecio umbellatus
A smooth perennial to 700 mm with undivided or slightly divided very narrow leaves up to 150 mm long with edges tightly rolled under, mainly on the lower stems. Thin branches with very much smaller leaves bear loose groups of magenta, pink or white heads about 15 mm across. They are enfolded below by 2 circles of bracts, the inner 3 times the length of the outer, some with papery edges. Occurring on flats and slopes from Ceres and Paarl to the Swartberg, and from the Cape Peninsula to Uitenhage. (Sept-Dec)

Senecio coleophyllus
A magnificent robust shrub to 2 m with sturdy woody stems and sparsely sharp-toothed leaves up to 90 mm by 20 mm. The showy flowerheads, up to 40 mm across, are borne in loose groups on cobwebby stalks and have 2 rows of woolly or hairless bracts, the outer shorter than the inner and alternately papery-edged. It occurs on mountain slopes, usually near water, in the Caledon district. (Sept-Jan)

Senecio cymbalariifolius
An erect, hairless perennial to 400 mm with tuberous roots, and very variable leaves mostly at the base of the plant. The lower ones are on long stalks, with much smaller, stalkless upper leaves partly enfolding the flowering stems. The flowering heads, about 30 mm across have a single row of loose narrow bracts, alternately papery-edged. Occurring on lower to midslopes from the Cedarberg to the Cape Peninsula and Caledon, it blooms profusely after fires. (Aug-Dec)

Two more smallish species have rosettes or tufts of rounded or broad, pointed leaves but yellow flowers: *S. cordifolius* of moist sheltered slopes, has delicate leaves often purple beneath, borne on branches which may become trailer-like; the sprawling *S. arniciflorus* of coastal sands has leathery leaves with a woolly reverse.

Anaxeton asperum
A straggly shrublet with woolly branches and harsh, almost prickly, narrow leaves 5-35 mm long, glossy green above and white woolly below. The flower-head, up to 35 mm across, consists of numerous individual posy-like groups each surrounded by a few outer buff-coloured hairy bracts. They appear deep red in bud, but open a dirty white. Occurring on sandy or stony mountainsides throughout this area from near sea level to 1 200 m. (Jan-Dec)

There are 9 species confined to the fynbos of which 3 occur in this area. The high altitude *A. ellipticum* has heart-shaped leaves; and *A. laeve* has smooth needlelike leaves.

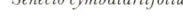

Senecio umbellatus

Senecio cymbalariifolius

Senecio coleophyllus

Anaxeton asperum

GLOSSARY

anther: pollen making terminal portion of a stamen. (Fig. 1)
annual: a plant growing from seed, blooming, making seeds and dying within one year.
axil: angle between stem and leafstalk. (Fig. 3)
bulb: underground storage and reproductive organ composed of succulent leaf bases or scales, e.g. onion.
bract: a modified leaf, for example, the reduced leaf on a flower stalk (Figs. 5, 7, 8); one of a large number surrounding the florets of a daisy. (Fig. 2)
calyx: the outermost circle of flower parts: the only parts visible before the flower opens, consisting of sepals which may be separate from one another (Fig. 1), or joined edge to edge to a greater or lesser extent.
compound: of a leaf, a group of several small lobes or leaflets making up one leaf (Fig. 4); of an inflorescence, a group of small flower clusters (Fig. 9).
corolla: the cirle of flower-parts immediately within the calyx, consisting of petals usually brightly coloured, which may be separate (Fig. 1), or to some extent joined edge to edge (Fig. 5).
corm: a swollen underground storage and reproductive organ derived from the base of a stem, e.g. Gladiolus.
toothed: having angular points which project outwards.
fynbos: used in a broad sense to designate the shrubby largely non-succulent vegetation of the winter rainfall mountains and the coastal belt down to the sea.
filament: the stalk of an anther, a part of the stamen (Fig. 1)
floret: a small flower, one of a mass crowded into a flowerhead (Fig. 2). As in Bruniaceae, Proteaceae and Asteraceae.
geophyte: a perennial plant with annual aboveground parts, persisting below ground during the dormant season in the form of a bulb, tuber or corm.
involucre: one or more series of bracts (modified reduced leaves) surrounding a flowerhead. (Fig. 2)
irregular: of a flower; the parts arranged unequally, unevenly around the centre (e.g. Lobelia, Sweet pea). (Figs. 5 & 7)
leaflet: one lobe or sub-unit of a compound leaf (Fig. 4)
lip: a group of petals together forming a structure different from the rest. (Fig. 5)
lobe: of a flower, the free terminal portion of a calyx or corolla (Fig. 5)
node: that section of a stem on which one or more leaves is attached. (Figs. 3, 4 & 8)
ovary: the seed-making innermost part of a flower (Fig. 1)
parasite: a plant lacking roots and attached to another rooted host plant, and drawing all or most of its nourishment from the host: usually containing little or no green plant pigment.
perianth: the outermost two circles of parts of a flower in which calyx and corolla are not clearly distinct, consisting of tepals (Figs. 6 & 7)
perennial: a plant which persists and blooms for several years.
petal: a lobe of the corolla (Fig. 1)

Fig. 1 Half-flower

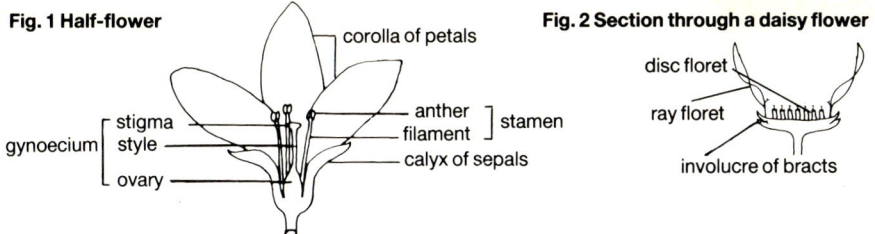

Fig. 2 Section through a daisy flower

Fig. 3 Simple leaf

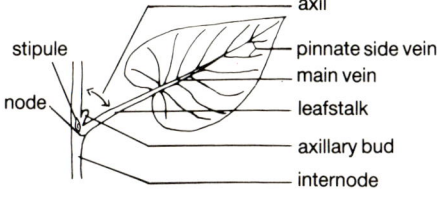

Fig. 4 Two kinds of compound leaf

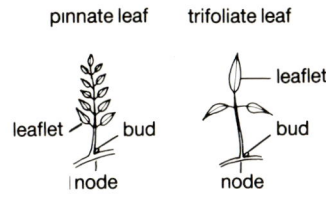

Fig. 5 Irregular flower

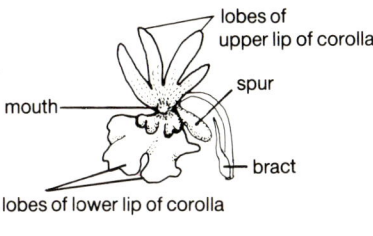

Fig. 6 Regular flower

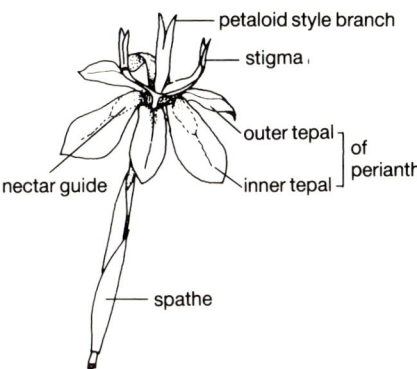

Fig. 7 Flower with a tube

Fig. 8 Spike inflorescence

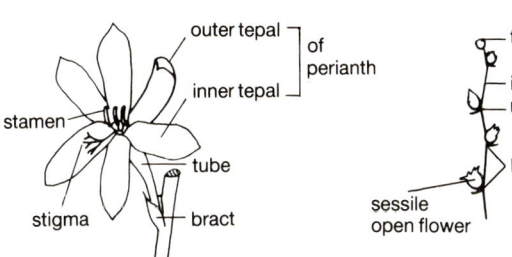

Fig. 9 Compound umbel inflorescence

pinnate: leaflets of a compound leaf (Fig. 4) or veins arising from a central vein like a double-sided comb. (Fig. 3)
ray floret: (of a daisy head) the outer, petal-like flowers (Fig. 2)
regular: of a flower: the parts evenly and equally distributed in a circle around the centre (see irregular) (Fig. 6)
sepal: calyx lobe or segment (Fig. 1)
sessile: having no stalk. (Fig. 8)
spike: A group of sessile flowers on an unbranched stem, with the youngest at the top (Fig. 8)
spur: a hollow pouch or tube formed from petals or sepals, containing nectar or oils to attract pollinating animals. (Fig. 5)
stamen: a unit of the male pollen-making part of a flower, consisting of anther and filament. (Figs. 1 & 7)
stigma: the pollen-receiving unit of a gynoecium (Figs. 1, 6 & 7) the female part of a flower.
stipule: an appendage of a leaf situated at the base of a leafstalk alongside the attachment of the leafstalk at a node; usually in pairs. (Fig. 3)
style: the stalk from the top of the ovary which carries the pollen-receptive stigma at its tip presents it in the place most likely to come in contact with pollen. (Fig. 1)
tepal: a sub-unit or lobe of the perianth in a monocotylednous plant. (Figs. 6 & 7)
tuber: An elongated, swollen, usually nearly horizontal storage root or stem of a geophyte.
tube: of a flower is that portion of the petals or tepals which is joined together. (Fig. 7)
umbel: a group of stalked flowers all arising from a single point (Fig. 9)

LILIACEAE:

The family name **Liliaceae** is used in this guide because it is familiar and widely known in South Africa. Recent studies suggest that this group consists of such a wide diversity of rather unrelated plants that it must be divided into many different families, the **Liliaceae** themselves being unrepresented in the South African flora. The new family names are given alongside the generic names: See **Veld & Flora** Sept. 1985. Vol. 71 No. 3.

Index to Botanical names

Adenandra acuta Schltr., 124
Adenandra brachyphylla Schldl., 124
Adenandra lasiantha Sonder, 124
Adenandra multiflora Strid, 124
Adenandra villosa (Berg.) Lichtenst.
　ex R. & S., 124
Adenandra viscida E. & Z., 124
Adromischus caryophyllaceus (Burm. f.)
　Lemaire, 100
Adromischus hemisphaericus (L.) Lemaire,
　100
Agapanthus africanus (L.) Hoffsgg., 30
Agapanthus walshii L. Bolus, 30
Agathelpis dubia (L.) Hutch, 172
Agathosma juniperifolia Bart., 124
AIZOACEAE, 92
Aizoon sarmentosum L.f., 92
Albuca canadensis (L.) Leighton, 30
Albuca cooperi Baker, 30
Albuca fragrans Jacq., 30
ALLIACEAE, 30
AMARYLLIDACEAE, 40-44
Amaryllis belladonna L., 44
ANACARDIACEAE, 130
Anapalina burchellii N.E. Br., 44
Anapalina nervosa (Thunb.) G. Lewis, 44
Anapalina pulchra (Baker) N.E. Br., 44
Anapalina triticea (Burm. f.) N.E. Br., 44
Anaxeton asperum (Thunb.) DC., 206
Anaxeton ellipticum Lundgren, 206
Anaxeton laeve (Harvey) Lundgren, 206
Anemone tenuifolia (L.f.) DC., 96
　(=A. capensis)
Anisodontea scabrosa (L.) D. Bates, 134
Anomalesia cunonia (L.) N.E. Br., 46
APIACEAE, 142-146
APONOGETONACEAE, 24
Aponogeton distachyos L.f., 24
Arctopus echinatus L., 146
Arctopus monacanthus Carmichael ex
　Sonder, 146
Argyrolobium filiforme (Thunb.) E. & Z., 108
Argyrolobium lunare (L.) Druce, 108
Aristea major Andrews, 46
　(=A. thyrsiflora)
Aristea oligocephala Baker, 46
Aristea racemosa Baker, 46
Aristea spiralis (L.f.) Ker Gawl., 46
Aristea zeyheri Baker, 46
ASCLEPIADACEAE, 162
Asclepias cancellata Burm. f., 162
Asclepias fruticosa L., 162
Aspalathus ciliaris L., 110
Aspalathus crenata (L.) Dahl., 108
Aspalathus excelsa Dahl., 110

Aspalathus laricifolia Berg., 110
ASPARAGACEAE, 38
ASPHODELACEAE, 30,32,36
ASTERACEAE, 182-206
Athanasia parviflora L., 204
Aulax cancellata (L.) Druce, 76
Aulax pallasia Stapf, 76
Aulax umbellata (Thunb.) R. Br., 76

Babiana ambigua (R. & S.) G. Lewis, 48
Babiana montana G. Lewis, 48
Babiana patersoniae L. Bolus, 48
Babiana purpurea (Jacq.) Ker Gawl., 48
Babiana stricta (Aiton) Ker Gawl., 48
BALANOPHORACEAE, 90
Berkheya barbata (L.f.) Hutch., 202
Berkheya herbacea (L.f.) Druce, 202
Berkheya rigida (Thunb.) A. & S., 202
Berzelia ecklonii Pill., 102
Berzelia incurva Pill., 102
Berzelia lanuginosa (L.) Brongn., 102
Berzelia rubra (Willd.) Schldl., 102
Berzelia squarrosa (Thunb.) Sonder, 102
Bobartia filiformis (L.f.) Ker Gawl., 48
Bobartia longicyma Gillett, 48
Bonatea speciosa (L.f.) Willd., 70
BORAGINACEAE, 162
BRASSICACEAE, 96
BRUNIACEAE, 102-106
Brunia albiflora E. Phillips, 104
Brunia alopecuroides Thunb., 102
Brunia laevis Thunb., 104
Brunia neglecta Schltr., 104
Brunia nodiflora L., 106
Brunia stokoei E. Phillips, 106
Brunsvigia marginata (Jacq.) Aiton, 42
　(=Nerine marginata)
Brunsvigia orientalis (L.) Aiton ex Ecklon, 42
Bulbine frutescens (L.) Willd., 32
Bulbine lagopus (Thunb.) N.E. Br., 32
Bulbinella floribunda (Aiton) D. & S., 32
Bulbinella triquetra (L.f.) Kunth, 32

CAMPANULACEAE, 174-182
Cannomois virgata (Rottb.) Steud., 28
Carpobrotus acinaciformis (L.) L. Bolus, 94
Carpobrotus edulis (L.) N.E. Br., 94
Carpobrotus pillansii L. Bolus, 94
Cassytha ciliolata Nees, 96
Castalis nudicaulis (L.) Norlindh, 194
CELASTRACEAE, 130
Centella difformis (E. & Z.) Adamson, 144
Centella triloba (Thunb.) Drude, 144
Ceratocaryum argenteum Kunth, 28
Chironia baccifera L., 160

211

Chironia decumbens Levyns, 160
Chironia jasminoides L., 160
Chironia linoides L., 160
Chironia melampyrifolia Lam., 160
Chironia stokoei Verdoorn, 160
Chironia tetragona L.f., 160
Chlorophytum rigidum Kunth, 30
Chlorophytum undulatum (Jacq.) Oberm., 30
Chrysanthemoides incana (Burm. f.) Norlindh, 192
Chrysanthemoides monilifera (L.) Norlindh, 192
Cliffortia multiformis Weim., 108
Cliffortia ruscifolia L., 108
Clutia alaternoides L., 128
Clutia polygonoides L., 128
Clutia pubescens Thunb., 128
Clutia rubricaulis E. & Z. ex Sonder, 128
COLCHICACEAE, 32,34
COMMELINACEAE, 30
Commelina africana L., 30
Commelina benghalensis L., 30
Corymbium africanum L., 184
Corymbium congestum E. Meyer ex DC., 184
Corymbium villosum L.f., 184
Cotyledon orbiculata L., 100
CRASSULACEAE, 100
Crassula coccinea L., 100
Crassula fascicularis Lam., 100
 (=Rochea subulata)
Crassula obtusa Haw., 100
Cyclopia falcata (Harvey) Kies, 108
Cyclopia genistoides (L.), Vent., 108
Cyclopia maculata (Andrews) Kies, 108
CYPERACEAE, 24
Cyphia bulbosa (L.) Bergius, 176
Cyphia digitata (Thunb.) Willd., 176
Cyphia phyteuma (L.) Willd., 176
Cyphia volubilis (Burm. f.) Willd., 176
Cyrtanthus angustifolius (L.f.) Aiton, 40
Cyrtanthus carneus Lindley, 40
Cyrtanthus leucanthus Schltr., 40
Cyrtanthus ventricosus (Jacq.) Willd., 40
Cytinus capensis Marloth, 168
Cytinus sanguineus (Thunb.) Fourc., 168

Diastella divaricata (Bergius) Rourke, 76
Diastella fraterna Rourke, 76
Diastella thymelaeoides (Bergius) Rourke, 76
Dilatris corymbosa Bergius, 40
Dilatris pillansii W. Barker, 40
Dilatris viscosa L.f., 40
DIPSACACEAE, 174
Disa pillansii L. Bolus, 68
Disa tripetaloides (L.f.) N.E. Br., 74
Disa uniflora Bergius, 68
Disa vaginata Lindley, 68

Dischisma arenarium E. Meyer, 172
Dischisma capitatum (Thunb.) Choisy, 172
Dischisma ciliatum (Bergius) Choisy, 172
Disparago lasiocarpa Cass., 182
Disperis capensis (L.f.) Sw., 74
Drimia elata Jacq. ex Willd., 32
Drimia forsteri (Baker) Oberm., 32
Drimia media Jacq. ex Willd., 32
DROSERACEAE, 98
Drosera acaulis L.f., 98
Drosera aliciae Raym.-Hamet, 98
Drosera capensis L., 98
Drosera cistiflora L., 98
Drosera glabripes (Harvey) Stein, 98
Drosera hilaris Cham. & Schldl., 98
Drosera ramentacea Burchell ex DC., 98
Drosera trinervia Spreng., 98

Echiostachys ecklonianus (Buek) Levyns, 162
Echiostachys incanus (Thunb.) Levyns, 162
Edmondia pinifolia (Lam.) Hilliard, 186
 (=Helichrysum pinifolia)
Edmondia sesamoides (L.) Willd., 200
 (=Helichrysum sesamoides)
Elegia capensis (Burm. f.) Schelpe, 28
Elegia equisetacea (Masters) Masters, 28
Elegia filacea Masters, 26
 (=E. parviflora)
Elegia persistens Pill., 26
Erepsia anceps (Haw.) L. Bolus, 92
Erepsia inclaudens (Haw.) Schwantes, 92
ERICACEAE, 146-156
Erica aristata Andrews, 152
Erica cerinthoides L., 146
Erica coccinea L., 156
Erica cruenta Sol., 156
Erica cumuliflora Salisb., 146
Erica fastigiata L., 148
Erica foliacea Andrews, 150
Erica grandiflora L.f., 150
Erica holosericea Salisb., 148
Erica imbricata L., 148
Erica irbyana Andrews, 152
Erica lanuginosa Andrews, 146
Erica longiaristata Benth., 154
Erica longifolia Aiton, 156
Erica mammosa L., 156
Erica massonii L.f., 152
Erica nana Salisb., 150
Erica onosmiflora Salisb., 156
Erica patersonia Andrews, 150
Erica perspicua Wendl., 148
Erica plukenetii L., 156
Erica pulchella Houtt, 154
Erica racemosa Thunb., 154
Erica retorta Montin, 152
Erica sessiliflora L.f., 154

Erica sphaeroidea Dulfer, 154
Erica subdivaricata Bergius, 154
Erica tenax L. Bolus, 150
Erica thomae L. Bolus, 150
Erodium incarnatum (L.) L'Her., 118
Eulophia litoralis Schltr., 70
EUPHORBIACEAE, 128
Euphorbia erythrina Link, 128
Euphorbia foliosa N.E. Br., 128
Euphorbia silenifolia (Haw.) Sweet, 128
 (=E. elliptica)
Euphorbia tuberosa L., 128
Euryops abrotanifolius (L.) DC., 202

FABACEAE, 108-116
Felicia aethiopica (Burm. f.) A. & S., 198
Felicia tenella (L.) Nees, 188
Ferraria crispa Burm., 66
FRANKENIACEAE, 136
Frankenia pulverulenta L., 136
Frankenia repens (Bergius) Fourc., 136

Gazania krebsiana Less., 184
Gazania pectinata (Thunb.) Sprengel, 184
Geissorhiza aspera Goldbl., 50
Geissorhiza ovata (Burm. f.) Asch. & Graeb., 50
Geissorhiza tenella Goldbl., 50
 (=Engysiphon roseus)
GENTIANACEAE. 158-160
GERANIACEAE, 118
Gerbera crocea (L.) Kuntze, 198
Gerbera linnaei Cass., 198
Gerbera piloselloides (L.) Cass., 198
Gerbera tomentosa DC., 198
Gladiolus acuminatus Bolus f., 54
Gladiolus blommesteinii L. Bolus, 50
Gladiolus brevifolius Jacq., 54
Gladiolus bullatus Thunb. ex G. Lewis, 52
Gladiolus carmineus C.H. Wright, 52
Gladiolus carneus Delaroche, 52
Gladiolus debilis Ker Gawl, 52
Gladiolus gracilis Jacq., 54
Gladiolus liliaceus Houtt., 54
Gladiolus maculatus Sweet, 54
Gladiolus ornatus Klatt, 50
Gladiolus pillansii G. Lewis, 54
Gladiolus punctulatus Schrank, 54
Gladiolus undulatus L., 52
Gladiolus vaginatus Bolus f., 54
Gnidia chrysophylla Meiss., 142
Gnidia juniperifolia Lam., 140
Gnidia laxa (L.f.) Gilg, 142
Gnidia oppositifolia L., 140
Gnidia pinifolia L., 140
Gnidia spicata (L.f.) Gilg, 142

Gnidia squarrosa (L.) Druce, 142
 (=G. polystachya)
Gnidia tomentosa L., 140
GRUBBIACEAE, 90
Grubbia rosmarinifolia Bergius, 90
Grubbia rourkei Carlq., 90
Grubbia tomentosa (Thunb.) Harms., 90
Gymnodiscus capillaris (L.f.) Less., 202

Haemanthus canaliculatus Levyns, 42
Haemanthus coccineus L., 42
Haemanthus sanguineus Jacq., 42
 (=H. rotundifolius)
HAEMODORACEAE, 38-40
Halleria elliptica Thunb., 166
Halleria lucida L., 166
Haplocarpha lanata (Thunb.) Less., 190
Harveya bolusii Kuntze, 168
Harveya capensis Hook., 168
Harveya laxiflora Hiern, 168
Harveya purpurea (L.f.) Harvey, 168
Harveya tubulosa Harvey ex Hiern, 168
 (=H. coccinea)
Hebenstreitia, 172
Helichrysum felinum (Thunb.) Less., 200
Helichrysum foetidum (L.) Moench, 200
Helichrysum retortum (L.) Willd., 186
Helichrysum stoloniferum (L.f.) Willd., 186
Helichrysum vestitum (L.) Schrank, 186
Heliophila linearis (Thunb.) DC., 96
Heliophila macra Schltr., 96
Helipterum zeyheri Sonder, 200
Hemimeris racemosa (Houtt.) Merill, 170
 (=H. montana)
Hemimeris sabulosa L.f., 170
Hermannia rudis N.E. Br., 134
Hermannia ternifolia Presl ex Harvey, 136
Hermannia sp., 134
Hermas ciliata L.f., 144
Hermas gigantea L.f., 144
Hermas quercifolia E. & Z., 144
Hermas quinquedentata L.f., 144
Hermas villosa (L.) Thunb., 144
Herschelianthe graminifolia (Ker Gawl. ex Spreng.) Rausch., 68
Herschelianthe purpurascens (H. Bol.) Rausch., 68
Hesperantha falcata (L.f.) Ker Gawl., 56
Heterolepis aliena (L.f.) Druce, 202
Heterolepis peduncularis DC., 202
Heteroptilis suffruticosa (Bergius) Lente, 142
Hibiscus aethiopicus L., 134
Hibiscus diversifolius Jacq., 134
Hibiscus trionum L., 134
Hippia frutescens (L.) L., 204
Homeria bulbillifera G. Lewis, 56
HYACINTHACEAE, 30, 32, 34, 36

Hyobanche sanguinea L., 168
Hypocalyptus coluteoides (Lam.) Dahl., 112
Hypocalyptus oxalidifolius (Sims) Baillon, 112
Hypocalyptus sophoroides (Berg.) Baillon, 112
HYPOXIDACEAE, 44

Indigofera filifolia Thunb, 112
Indigofera mauritanica (L.) Thunb., 112
Indigofera sarmentosa L.f., 112
IRIDACEAE, 44-66
Ixia cochlearis G. Lewis, 56
Ixia dubia Vent., 56
Ixia flexuosa L., 56
Ixia micrandra Baker, 56
Ixia odorata Ker Gawl., 56
Ixia trinervata (Baker) G. Lewis, 56

Lachenalia bulbifera (Cirillo) Hort., 34
Lachenalia fistulosa W. Barker, 34
Lachenalia orchioides (L.) Aiton, 34
Lachenalia peersii Marloth ex W. Barker, 34
Lachenalia rosea Andrews, 34
Lachenalia rubida Jacq., 34
Lachnaea densiflora Meissner, 138
LAMIACEAE, 164
Lampranthus antemeridianus (L. Bol.) L. Bol., 94
Lampranthus bicolor (L.) N.E. Br., 94
Lampranthus calcaratus (Wolley-Dod) N.E. Br., 92
Lampranthus furvus (L. Bolus) N.E. Br., 92
Lampranthus filicaulis (Haw.) N.E. Br., 92
Lampranthus glaucus (L.) N.E. Br., 94
Lampranthus reptans (Sol.) N.E. Br., 94
Lampranthus wordsworthiae (L. Bolus) N.E. Br., 92
Lanaria lanata (L.) D. & S., 40
Lapeirousia corymbosa (L.) Ker Gawl., 62
LAURACEAE, 96
Laurophyllus capensis Thunb., 130
Lebeckia grandiflora Benth., 114
Lebeckia pauciflora E. & Z., 114
Lebeckia simsiana E. & Z., 114
Lebeckia wrightii (Harvey) Bolus, 114
Leucadendron gandogeri Schinz ex Gand., 80
Leucadendron rubrum Burm. f., 78
Leucadendron spissifolium (Salisb. ex Knight) I.J. Williams, 78
Leucadendron tinctum I.J. Williams, 78
Leucospermum gracile (Salisb. ex Knight) Rourke, 82
Leucospermum gueinzii Meissner, 82
Leucospermum hypophyllocarpodendron (L.) Druce, 82

Leucospermum lineare R. Br., 82
Leucospermum oleifolium (Bergius) R. Br., 80
Leucospermum prostratum (Thunb.) Stapf, 82
Leucospermum truncatulum (Salisb. ex Knight) Rourke, 84
Lichtensteinia lacera Cham. & Schldl., 144
Lightfootia diffusa Buek, 178
LILIACEAE, 30-38
Limonium anthericoides (Schltr.) Dyer, 158
Limonium depauperatum (Boiss.) Dyer, 158
Limonium kraussianum (Buchinger ex Boiss.) Kuntze, 158
Limonium scabrum (Thunb.) Kuntze, 158
LINACEAE, 122
Linum africanum L., 122
Linum quadrifolium L., 122
Linum thunbergii E. & Z., 122
Liparia splendens (Burm. f.) Bos & De Wit, 110
Lobelia chamaepitys Lam., 176
Lobelia coronopifolia L., 176
Lobelia jasionoides (A. DC.) Wimmer, 174
Lobelia linearis Thunb., 178
Lobelia pubescens Aiton, 176
Lobelia setacea Thunb., 178
Lobelia tomentosa L.f., 176
Lobostemon fruticosus (L.) Buek, 162

Mairea corymbosa Harvey, 198
MALVACEAE, 134
Manulea cheiranthus L., 170
Manulea leiostachys Benth., 170
Manulea minor Diels, 172
Manulea tomentosa L., 170
  (=M. rubra)
Mariscus thunbergii (Vahl) Schrader, 24
  (=M. riparius)
Melasma scabrum Bergius, 168
Merciera brevifolia A. DC., 178
Merciera eckloniana Buek, 178
Merciera leptoloba A. DC., 178
Merciera tenuifolia (L.f.) A. DC., 178
Merciera vaginata Adamson, 178
MESEMBRYANTHEMACEAE, 92-94
Metalasia cephalotes (Thunb.) Less., 194
Metalasia muricata (L.) D. Don, 194
Mimetes cucullatus (L.) R. Br., 80
Mimetes hirtus (L.) Salisb. ex Knight, 80
Monadenia comosa Reichb. f., 74
Monopsis lutea (L.) Urb., 182
Monopsis simplex (L.) F. Wimmer, 182
Moraea angusta (Thunb.) Ker Gawl., 58
Moraea anomala G. Lewis, 58
Moraea bellendenii (Sweet) N.E. Br., 58, 60
Moraea bituminosa (L.f.) Ker Gawl., 58
Moraea ciliata (L.F.) Ker Gawl., 60

Moraea fugax (Delaroche) Jacq., 60
Moraea lugubris (Salisb.) Goldbl., 58
Moraea neglecta G. Lewis, 60
Moraea papilionacea (L.f.) Ker Gawl., 60
Moraea tricolor Andrews, 60
Moraea tricuspidata (L.f.) G. Lewis, 58
Moraea tripetala (L.f.) Ker Gawl., 58
Moraea villosa (Ker Gawl.) Ker Gawl., 60
Moraea viscaria (L.f.) Ker Gawl., 58
Muraltia ericoides (Burm. f.) Steudel, 126
Mystropetalon polemannii Harvey, 90
Mystropetalon thomii Harvey, 90

Nebelia fragarioides (Willd.) Kuntze, 106
Nebelia paleacea (Bergius) Sweet, 106
Nebelia sphaerocephala (Sonder) Kuntze, 106
Nemesia versicolor E. Meyer ex Benth., 166
Nerine humilis (Jacq.) Herbert, 42
Nerine sarniensis (L.) Herbert, 42
Nivenia concinna N.E. Br., 60
Nivenia levynsiae Weim., 60
Nivenia stokoei N.E. Br., 60

Oedera capensis (L.) Druce, 196
Oedera imbricata Lam., 196
Oldenbergia intermedia Bond ined., 198
Oldenbergia paradoxa Less., 198
OLEACEAE, 158
Olea exasperata Jacq., 158
Onixotis punctata (L.) Mabberley, 32
 (=Dipidax punctata)
Onixotis triquetra (L.f.) Mabberley, 32
 (=Dipidax triquetra)
ORCHIDACEAE, 68-74
Ornithogalum dubium Houtt., 36
Ornithogalum esterhuyseniae Oberm., 36
Ornithogalum graminifolium Thunb., 36
Ornithogalum hispidum Hornem., 36
Ornithogalum juncifolium Jacq., 36
Ornithogalum thyrsoides Jacq., 36
Orphium frutescens (L.) E. Meyer, 158
Osmitopsis asteriscoides (Bergius) Less., 192
Osmitopsis parvifolia (DC.) Hofmeyer, 192
Osteospermum polygaloides L., 196
Osteospermum rotundifolium (DC.) Norl., 196
Osteospermum tomentosum (L.f.) Norl., 196
Otholobium obliquum (E. Meyer) Stirton, 114
Othonna dentata L., 190
Othonna parviflora Bergius, 190
Othonna quinquedentata Thunb., 192
OXALIDACEAE, 118-122
Oxalis corniculata L., 120
Oxalis dentata Jacq., 118
Oxalis eckloniana Presl, 122
Oxalis luteola Jacq., 120
Oxalis multicaulis E. & Z., 120

Oxalis polyphylla Jacq., 120
Oxalis purpurea L., 120
Oxalis tenuifolia Jacq., 120
Oxalis truncatula Jacq., 122

Pelargonium cucullatum (L.) L'Her., 118
Pelargonium myrrhifolium (L.) L'Her., 118
PENAEACEAE, 136-138
Penaea cneorum Meerb., 136
Penaea mucronata L., 136
Peucedanum galbanum (L.) Benth. & Hook. f., 142
Phaenocoma prolifera (L.) D. Don, 186
Phylica ericoides L., 130
Phylica gracilis (E. & Z.) Dietr., 132
Phylica lasiocarpa Sonder, 132
Phylica plumosa L., 132
Phylica pubescens Aiton, 132
Phylica spicata L.f., 132
Pillansia templemanii L. Bolus, 64
PLUMBAGINACEAE, 158
POACEAE, 24
Podalyria calyptrata Willd., 112
Polyarrhena reflexa (L.) Cass., 190
Polyarrhena stricta Gran, 190
POLYGALACEAE, 126
Polygala bracteolata L., 126
Polygala garcini DC., 126
Polygala meridionalis Levyns, 126
Polygala myrtifolia L., 126
Polygala umbellata L., 126
Priestleya calycina L. Bolus, 114
Priestleya vestita (Thunb.) DC., 114
Prismatocarpus diffusus (L.f.) A. DC., 182
Protasparagus aethiopicus (L.) Oberm., 38
Protasparagus rubicundus (Bergius) Oberm., 38
PROTEACEAE, 76-88
Protea acaulos (L.) Reichard, 84
Protea burchellii Stapf, 86
 (=P. pulchra)
Protea compacta R. Br., 86
Protea cynaroides (L.) L., 84
Protea laurifolia Thunb., 86
Protea longifolia Andrews, 84
Protea neriifolia R. Br., 86
Protea speciosa L., 86
Protea stokoei E. Phillips, 86
Pseudobaeckia africana (Burm. f.) Pill., 104
Pseudobaeckia cordata (Burm. F.) Niedenzu, 104
Pseudobaeckia stokoei Pill., 104
Pseudopentameris brachyphylla (Stapf) Conert, 24
Psoralea aphylla L., 116
Psoralea pinnata L., 116
Pterocelastrus rostratus (Thunb.) Walp., 130

215

Pterocelastrus tricuspidatus (Lam.) Sonder, 130
Pteronia camphorata (L.) L., 184
Pteronia hirsuta L.f., 184
Pteronia scabra Harvey, 184
Pteronia tenuifolia DC., 184
Pterygodium alatum (Thunb.) Sw., 74
Pterygodium catholicum (L.) Sw., 70

RAFFLESIACEAE, 168
RANUNCULACEAE, 96
Raspalia globosa (Lam.) Pill., 106
Raspalia microphylla (Thunb.) Brongn., 106
Raspalia phylicoides (Thunb.) Arnott, 106
Raspalia variabilis Pill., 106
Raspalia virgata (Brongn.) Pill., 106
Rafnia cuneifolia Thunb., 114
RESTIONACEAE, 26-28
RETZIACEAE, 166
Retzia capensis Thunb., 166
RHAMNACEAE, 130-132
Rhus laevigata L., 130
Rhynchosia ferulifolia Benth. ex Harvey, 116
Roella arenaria Schltr., 180
Roella ciliata L., 180
Roella incurva A. DC., 180
Roella maculata Adamson, 180
Roella prostrata E. Meyer ex A. DC., 180
Romulea hirsuta (Ecklon ex Klatt) Baker, 62
Romulea rosea (L.) Ecklon, 62
Romulea triflora (Burm. f.) N.E. Br., 62
RORIDULACEAE, 98
Roridula gorgonias Planchon, 98
ROSACEAE, 108
Ruschia leptophylla L. Bolus, 94
Ruschia macowanii (L. Bolus) Schwantes, 94
Ruschia sarmentosa (Haw.) Schwantes, 94
Ruschia stokoei L. Bolus, 94
RUTACEAE, 124

Saltera sarcocolla (L.) Bullock, 138
Salvia africana-caerulea L., 164
Salvia africana-lutea L., 164
Salvia chamelaeagnea Bergius, 164
SANTALACEAE, 90
Satyrium carneum (Dryander) Sims, 72
Satyrium coriifolium Sw., 72
Satyrium lupulinum Lindley, 72
Satyrium odorum Sonder, 72
Scabiosa columbaria L., 174
Schizodium obliquum Lindley, 70
SCROPHULARIACEAE, 166-172
SELAGINACEAE, 172-174
Selago incisa Hochst., 174
Selago scabrida Thunb., 174
Selago serrata Bergius, 174
Selago spuria L., 174

Selago thunbergii Choisy, 174
Selago verbenacea L.f., 174
Senecio arenarius Thunb., 182
Senecio arnicaeflorus DC., 206
Senecio coleophyllus Turcz., 206
Senecio cordifolius L.f., 206
Senecio cymbalariifolius (L.) Less., 206
Senecio elegans L., 182
Senecio pinifolius (L.) Lam., 204
Senecio triqueter Less., 204
Senecio umbellatus L., 206
Serruria adscendens (Lam.) R. Br., 88
Serruria elongata (Bergius) R. Br., 88
Serruria heterophylla Meissner, 88
Serruria phylicoides (Bergius) R. Br., 88
  (=S. barbigera)
Serruria rosea E. Phillips, 88
Serruria rubricaulis R. Br., 88
Siphocodon debilis Schltr., 180
Siphocodon spartioides Turcz., 180
SOLANACEAE, 166
Solanum guineense L., 166
Solanum quadrangulare Thunb. ex L.f., 166
Sonderothamnus petraeus (W. Barker) Dahl., 138
Sonderothamnus speciosus (Sonder) Dahl., 138
Sparaxis grandiflora (Delaroche) Ker Gawl., 64
Spatalla curvifolia Salisb. ex Knight, 76
Spatalla mollis R. Br., 76
Spatalla racemosa (L.) Druce, 76
Spiloxene aquatica (L.f.) Fourc., 44
Spiloxene capensis (L.) Garside, 44
Spiloxene flaccida (Nel) Garside, 44
Staavia brownii Dummer, 104
Staavia capitella (Thunb.) Sonder, 104
  (=S. comosa)
Staavia radiata (L.) Dahl., 104
Stachys aethiopica L. 164
STERCULIACEAE, 134-136
STILBACEAE, 162-164
Stilbe ericoides L., 162
Stilbe mucronata N.E., Br., 164
Stoebe cinerea Thunb., 204
Stoebe incana Thunb., 204
Stoebe plumosa (L.) Thunb., 204
Struthiola confusa C.H. Wright, 140
Struthiola eckloniana Meissner, 140
Struthiola martiana Meissner, 138
  (=S. fourcadei)
Struthiola mundii Ecklon ex Meissner, 138
Struthiola myrsinites Lam., 140
Struthiola salteri Levyns, 140
Struthiola striata Lam., 142
Struthiola tetralepis Schltr., 142
Struthiola tomentosa Andrews, 138
Sutera tristis (L.f.) Hiern, 170

Teedia lucida (Aiton) Rudolphi, 172
Tephrosia capensis (Jacq.) Pers., 116
Tetraria thermalis (L.) C.B. Clarke, 24
Thaminophyllum latifolium Bond, 190
Thereianthus bracteolatus (Lam.) G. Lewis, 66
Thereianthus juncifolius (Baker) G. Lewis, 66
Thereianthus spicatus (L.) G. Lewis, 66
Thesium carinatum A. DC., 90
Thesium euphorbioides L., 90
THYMELAEACEAE, 138-142
Trachyandra hirsutiflora (Adamson) Oberm., 36
Tritonia cooperi (Baker) Klatt, 62
Tritonia crispa (L.f.) Ker Gawl., 62
Tritonia flabellifolia (Delaroche) G. Lewis, 62
Tritoniopsis dodii (G. Lewis) G. Lewis, 66
Tritoniopsis lata (L. Bolus) G. Lewis, 66
Tritoniopsis pulchella G. Lewis, 66
Tritoniopsis ramosa Ecklon ex Klatt, 66

Ursinia caledonica (E. Phillips) Prassler, 188
Ursinia eckloniana (Sonder) N.E. Br., 188
Ursinia paleacea (L.) Moench, 188
 (=U. crithmoides)
Ursinia quinquepartita (DC.) N.E. Br., 188

Villarsia capensis (Houtt.) Merrill, 158
VIOLACEAE, 136
Viola decumbens L.f., 136

Wachendorfia brachyandra W. Barker, 38
Wachendorfia graminifolia L.f., 38
Wachendorfia paniculata L., 38
Wachendorfia thyrsiflora L., 38
Watsonia borbonica (Pourret) Goldbl., 66
 (=W. pyramidata)
Watsonia schlechteri L. Bolus, 64
Watsonia stenosiphon L. Bolus, 64
Wurmbea spicata (Burm. f.) D. & S., 34

Zaluzianskya capensis (L.) Walp., 168
Zaluzianskya villosa F.W. Schmidt, 170
ZYGOPHYLLACEAE, 122
Zygophyllum flexuosum E. & Z., 122
Zygophyllum fulvum L., 122
Zygophyllum sessilifolium L. 122

Index to Common names

Aandblom, 56
Aardboontjie, 176
Aardroos, 84
Aasuintjie, 56
Afrikaanse salie, 164
Agtdaegeneesbos, 162
Altydbossie, 104
Altydvygie, 92
April Fool, 42

Bastard Olive, 158
Basterolienhout, 158
Bekkies, 34
Belladonna lily, 44
Belskruie, 192
Bergaarbossie, 174
Bergajuin, 42
Bergbaroe, 176
Berggeelbos, 80
Berglelie, 42
Bergnaeltjie, 34
Bergpalmiet, 24
Bergroos, 84
Bergseldery, 142
Bergstompie, 106
Biesroei, 48
Bietou, 192
Bitterbos, 174
Blisterbush, 142
Blombos, 194
Blood flower, 42
Blouaarbossie, 174
Bloublommetjiesalie, 164
Blouertjieblom, 126
Bloukeur, 116
Bloulelie, 30
Blouviooltjie, 34
Blue Disa, 68
Boetabessie, 192
Boneseed bush, 192
Botrivier protea, 86
Bot River protea, 86
Bottle heath, 152
Botterblom, 64
Brandbossie, 190
Brown afrikander, 54
Bruin afrikander, 54
Brakblommetjie, 158
Bush honeysuckle, 166

Caledon bluebell, 52
Candelabra flower, 42
Cape edelweiss, 40
Cape flax, 122
Cat's tail, 172

Cherrywood, 130
Chincherinchee, 36
Climber's friend, 108
Coffee bush, 104
Crane's bill, 118
Crimson heath, 156

Devil's sewing thread, 96
Devil's tresses, 96
Doll's roses, 134
Doublom, 98
Drumsticks, 170
Duine-taaibos, 130
Dune taaibos, 130

Ertjieblom, 112
Everlasting, 186, 200
Ewwa-trewwa, 72

False cedar, 106
Featherhead, 132
Fire heath, 146
Fish bean, 116
Fluweelblom, 64
Fonteinbos, 116
Fonteinbossie, 106
Four sisters heath, 148
Froetang, 62

Gansies, 162
Geelmargriet, 188, 202
Geel tjienkerientjee, 36
Geldbeursie, 30
Ghombossie, 184
Giant protea, 84
Gombos, 184
Grootbiesie, 48
Groot suikerroos, 84
Guernsey lily, 42

Haakdoring, 38
Hanekammetjie, 32
Hangertjie, 156
Hermanus cliff gladiolus, 52
Heuningblom, 166
Heuningbossie, 184
Heuningtee, 108
Honey tea, 108
Horlosies, 118
Hotnotsvy, 94
Hottentots fig, 94

Inkblom, 168
Ink flower, 168
Iron martin, 130

Jeukbol, 32
Jeukbossie, 128

Kaffertjie, 34
Kalmoes, 144
Kalmus, 144
Kalossie, 56
Kapokblom, 40
Kapotjie, 70
Katbossie, 164
Katnaels, 168
Katoenbos, 162
Katstert, 32
Katstertjie, 142
Kersblakertjie, 58
Kershout, 130
Keurblom, 112
King protea, 84
Klipblom, 100, 110
Klipknopbossie, 102
Knikkertjies, 62
Koffiebos, 104
Koningskandelaar, 42
Koringblommetjie, 62
Kouteri, 100

Leafless pea, 112
Leeubekkie, 166
Little sundew, 98
Luibos, 162

Maagbossie, 46
Maartblom, 44
March lily, 44
Masson's heath, 152
Mealie heath, 150
Melkbol, 128
Moederkappie, 70, 74
Mountain dahlia, 110
Mountain daisy, 192

Nentabos, 100
Nooienshaar, 96
Notsung, 166

Oktoberlelie, 70
Orange nodding head, 110
Ox-eye daisy, 194

Painted lady, large, 52
Painted lady, small, 52
Patrysbos, 84
Peacock flower, 44
Penwortel, 116
Perdekapok, 40

Perdespookbossie, 42
Pienk satynblom, 50
Pig's ear, 100
Pink keurtjie, 112
Pink satin flower, 50
Pink ixia, 56
Pisgoed, 128
Plampers, 184
Platdoring, 146
Pokkiesdoring, 146
Poprosies, 134
Poublommetjie, 44
Prince of Wales heath, 148
Pypie, 54

Rankals, 204
Red crassula, 100
Red disa, 68
Roemenaggie, 138, 142
Rooiblombossie, 194
Rooidisa, 68
Rooihartjie, 146
Rooiheide, 156
Rooikanol, 38
Rooikeur, 112
Rooipypie, 46
Rooisewejaartjie, 186
Rooistompie, 106
Rooitrewwa, 72
Rooiwortel, 40
Ruiktrewwa, 72

Sandkalossie, 34
Scabious, 174
Sea heath, 136
Sea lavender, 158

Sea parsley, 142
Septemberbossie, 126
Sewejaartjie, 186, 200
Skaamblom, 110
Snail flower, 168
Sour fig, 94
Soldier-in-a-box, 30
Spiderbush, 102
Spinnekopblom, 38, 66
Sprawling pea, 112
Sprawling sundew, 98
Steekbos, 108
Sterretjie, 44
Stinkbos, 172
Stinksewejaartjie, 200
Stompie, 106
Strandblommetjie, 182
Strandsalie, 164
Strawberry everlasting, 200
Stream buchu, 124
Stream bush, 104
Strooiblommetjie, 200
Stroombos, 104
Suikerkannetjie, 46
Sundew, 98
Suurkanol, 66, 74
Suurvy, 94
Syblom, 50, 96
Sysie, 50

Tjienkerientjee, 36
Tolletjiesbos, 78
Tontelblaar, 144
Tontelblaarbossie, 198
Tontelblom, 186
Tree pelargonium, 118

Uiltjie, 66
Uintjiestulp, 56

Varksoor, 100
Veerkoppie, 132
Veertjie, 142
Verfblommetjie, 168
Vingersuring, 120
Vleigeelbos, 78
Vlieëbos, 98, 138
Volstruisies, 106
Vrouebossie, 118
Vygie, 92

Wandelende Jood, 30
Wandering Jew, 30
Waterblommetjie, 24
Wateruintjie, 24
Weeskindertjies, 166
Wild anemone, 96
Wild asparagus, 38
Wild cineraria, 182
Wild cotton, 162
Wild hyacinth, 34
Wild lobelia, 176
Wild sage, 164
Wilde aspersie, 38
Wilde aster, 190, 198
Wilde malva, 118
Wilde margriet, 194
Witbergpypie, 40
Witsteekbossie, 194
Wolwekos, 168

Yellow chincherinchee, 36
Yellow lobelia, 182
Ystermartiens, 130

NOTES

NOTES

NOTES

About the Botanical Society of South Africa

Founded in 1913 at the same time as Kirstenbosch Botanic Gardens the Botanical Society aims to interest the people of South Africa and other countries in the National Botanic Gardens. We also aim to educate members of the public in the cultivation, conservation and awareness of our unique indigenous flora.

ARE YOU A MEMBER?

The Botanical Society of South Africa is one of the largest, most effective organisations working to safeguard our veld and flora. If you are not already a member we invite you to join. There is something for everyone in the Society's wide range of activities, from hikes and walks to illustrated lectures, tours and conservation activism. Members receive the colourful and informative "Veld & Flora" magazine, free seeds of your choice annually from the Kirstenbosch seedlist, as well as free admission to all the national botanic gardens in South Africa.

By joining the Society you support those members who are willing to invest their time and expertise to protect our natural heritage for this and future generations. We need your membership and support. To join, please contact the Executive Secretary, Botanical Society of South Africa, Kirstenbosch, Claremont 7735 RSA. or telephone Cape Town (021) 771725.

Any donations or bequests made to the Botanical Society are free of donations and estate duty tax.

FAREWELL MY FRIEND

Farewell for now, take care my friend,
Ah! I know this busy life spin around, nae end,
some peace, wordcatcher, catching words for you,
rest, to be, ah! take a time, to read a few,
from dreams, wordcatcher,
I wish your troubles quell
For you, a book, as a coin in the wishing well.

The wordcatcher sleeps tonight.

Colin Demét